ATTACK YOUR EXPENSES

SCOTT MCDOWELL

PUBLISHED BY SCOTT M ECOMMERCE

INTRODUCTION

I was born into a normal family. Well... as normal as a family can be. We were part owners of a fast food business. Like many family businesses, we made a living rather than a fortune, and my family worked like owners for an employee's salary.

My parents were frugal with their money, saving what little they had to make a better life. They did have some good years, and during those, we felt rich. They had a good amount of savings and a nicer house than most people, but it didn't come easy.

They didn't get to this point because they earned more money than everyone else. They ended up like this because they sacrificed a lot. This gave them the freedom to live happily, without the fear of poverty and they were able to keep the money that they earned.

When I was a small child, they gave me a biscuit tin and some pennies to put in it. Sometimes, they would give me more pennies and let me happily put them in the tin. I liked it for some reason, I was a kid and I had something that represented value. I didn't spend those pennies, I looked forward to adding more to the tin. What I didn't realise at the time, was that they were getting me ready to save money. They used to say things to me like, "pennies make pounds."

They helped me create my very first good habit. The habit I made was more than just saving money, it was sacrificing something today for a better tomorrow.

Unfortunately, I only applied that discipline to saving my pennies and playing sports, I didn't really care about anything else. I was blind to the idea of investing at that age, and was delusional in thinking that I could win at life without a good financial education.

In my twenties, my body racked up the injuries. I had to stop playing sports, which was my whole life at that point. I didn't have a passion for anything else.

One day, I decided to read a book recommended by the motivational speaker, Bob Proctor, called *Think and Grow Rich*. The pages of those books gave me an insight that I hadn't seen before, it lit a fire in me, I was no longer a broken ex-athlete, I had something to set my sights on, I was motivated with the ideas in the book. They pushed me to dream of being a millionaire, making my thoughts into reality, and having complete financial freedom.

I have tried many things, mostly online businesses, internet marketing and drop shipping but didn't have much luck. In fact, the first business that I ever started ended up landing me as a victim of fraud. In the end, I stumbled upon real estate investing books and began to study everything I could. It probably took me around a year to make my first investment, but that didn't matter. The first investment I made paved the way for many future investments, and changed my life in the process.

Over the years I continued to buy property to rent out, made profits from selling and repeated the process. I'm still not a millionaire, but I'm a lot closer. I made my first investment on a very average income and made some very simple choices. Literally, anyone can do what I have done.

Everything takes time but I promise you, this is within reach. You can be the first person in your family to become a millionaire and once you've reached that point, you can do what you want, where you want, and with whoever you choose to do it with.

Let's get you saving money and out of debt so you can move onto bigger and more exciting things. I wish you the best of luck.

WHY CUT EXPENSES?

Are you a slave to someone else's fortune, or the master of your own financial future?

This book is one of financial opportunities created through choices, and it will allow you to open up your life to amazing adventures, no matter the place you currently find yourself in.

Let's try and turn your whole financial world around.

Most books about saving money only talk about shrinking your life and doing less, rather than expanding your life's potential and offering many of the possibilities available to you. It's a shame we are taught to retreat when facing financial difficulties when this attitude can be self defeating.

Going to war with your financial World and trying new things is what is required, with your head held high ready to do what is necessary. Being open to change, willing to work and strategise like you never have before, to attain new virtues on this journey like being frugal and maintaining self control.

There are amazing benefits to being frugal. Being frugal does not mean cheap. Being Frugal just means not wasting precious resources on things that don't improve your life, happiness, health and wealth.

Whether you make a million dollars, or minimum wage, you should adopt the practice of spending less than you make.

There is not a single person who should be unconcerned about how they are spending money. It's not about having more money to spend - it's about making sure that you're getting your money's worth when you do.

. . .

YOU DON'T HAVE to be cheap, but you have to be mindful about how you deploy your capital. That is what frugality is all about. See how far your dollars can stretch and make the most out of the money you have worked so hard to earn.

IF ALL GOES WELL, you will be exchanging your old ways of doing things for new, more lucrative ways. Enhance your financial status and progress yourself towards a better way of life. Money can't buy happiness, but it can buy peace of mind.

HOW WOULD your life be if you had no expenses? What could you do with your time? Where would you go? Who would you spend time with? How could your life change for the better?

OF COURSE, you won't be able to completely cut out all the expenses in life. There are some who might be able to, but then it gets to a point where you're cutting out more than just money spent. You are cutting out the experiences, wellness, and joy that money can help you find. Still, there are ways you can drastically reduce the purchases you make. How would your life be if you had 50% fewer expenses? Or 25% fewer expenses?

THIS THOUGHT experiment makes you really consider how you are approaching your life. Make no mistake, your spending habits can hurt your quality of life.

WE SOMETIMES THINK that buying things will make us happy, but it can often lead to more financial stress. If we don't have the money to buy the essentials and have a safety net, we need to start thinking differently.

WITH THE FOLLOWING INFORMATION, you are going to learn how you can drive your cost of living down to the smallest amount possible whilst still enjoying your life.

YOU WILL LEARN all about the amazing things you can do with very little money, and enjoy a World full of possibilities, travel, entertainment, and the greatest gift of all; freedom, time, and peace of mind.

. . .

The Spinning Plates of Personal Finance

If you want a life filled with everything you dream of, less stress, and more freedom, then you will have to approach your financial situation using the four spinning plates of personal finance. This book deals with the first 2 plates, and some of the third. The fourth plate can be found in other books but we will focus more on the first 3. Taxes could be considered a 5th plate but I am not qualified to speak on that topic.

What Are The 4 Spinning Plates?

1. Destroy Debt
2. Save Money
3. Capital Allocation
4. Money Creation

Destroying debt is an obvious place to start your war on personal finances. The more personal debt you have, the faster you have to spin the other plates. It's like a treadmill that sets its own pace with you onboard. If you don't pay attention to debt, you'll always be running.

Save money! It sounds so boring, but it's not as bad as it seems. Having a large sum of money in your bank account gives you a feeling of stability in your life. Your emotions don't spike as much when something goes wrong. If your car breaks down when you're rich, it might be an inconvenience, but you don't get too stressed, you just pay it away. To feel like this, you need to have savings ready for when disaster strikes.

Capital allocation is a fancy way of saying spending wisely and investing wisely. It's something you imagine great titans of industry participating in, but the truth is, this skill is vital for everyone. Knowing what to spend your money on and how to invest, puts food on the table and pays for the shelter that shields you from the cold and keeps you safe.

You could say it's even more vital a skill for the poor to acquire than the rich. The rich aren't going to lose their home or starve. The irony of what I just said is that - the rich are usually rich because of their capital allocation skills. Unfortunately, they don't teach you that in public school.

Money creation is a powerful plate that can keep the other plates spinning much easier. How do we make money? And why do some people make fortunes when others make less than a living? We all generally work the same hours and some of the rich hardly work at all. Society hints at why these millionaires are paid more than the rest of us, but it's not a plain and simple answer. The rich don't get paid by the hour!

We are paid for the value we serve to a customer in product or service. The value of the product or service is decided in multiple ways, but ends with the decision of the buyer to say yes or no to the price.

To increase the value, or create something of value, there are many factors to consider.

Here are just some of them:

1. The products and services ideally are non-substitutable.
2. The products are rare.
3. The products are inimitable.
4. The product is easy to use.
5. The product is a time saver.
6. The product is highly functional, well designed, and packaged.

There are many other factors, but we couldn't

possibly list them all here. We want to sell a high volume of products, high priced products, and services all within a complete product line that works together.

When we have a product line worthy of selling, we need to use leverage to distribute and grow our operations. We do this by leveraging employees, online automated stores, marketplaces. We are leveraging machines and other companies to produce our products and anything else we can do, to make it possible to deliver our product/service.

We use loans and other people's money to help us start or grow our businesses. Sometimes, we sell shares to raise money for the company.

You can use your own money, but your chances of success will be enhanced or diminished by the amount of money you raise to complete your project. The terms of loans taken can also make or break a business. In the end it all banks on your company's ability to pay down debt and your company's ability to sell those products and services.

. . .

As mentioned earlier, the 4th plate is not what most of this book teaches, but it is worth learning about throughout your life.

All four of the plates are needed to become rich, and stay rich. It's basically the path from rags to riches. Each skill that improves, helps others become more stable and easier to control.

If you increase your money creation at the same rate you take on personal debt, you're not making much progress.

If you make money and don't keep any savings for when disaster comes, your investments will not save you. Especially if you can't gain access to the funds right away. Some assets are easier to liquidate than others, so take this into account.

If you can get down to zero personal debt, have savings in your bank, become a spending and investment master, and a money creation expert, you will sleep well and find complete financial freedom. After all, what is rich to one person may be poor to another, and vice versa.

. . .

Being rich isn't about just getting money. Anyone can find a way to make money, and there are a million ways to become a millionaire. If you want to be rich, you have to learn how to save and spend your money properly. It's really as simple as that.

Throughout this book, we are going to dive into all the random little ways to save your money. You can participate in every single one of these, or you can just pick and choose what is applicable to your life. We don't have to give up on the things that make us happy. We simply have to look for ways to be happy with what we have, not spending money on unnecessary things.

There's more to life than money, but life can be hard when we don't know how to properly navigate the financial world.

The Long-Term Effects of Spending Recklessly

If you're not careful, you will start to feel the long-term effects, of spending your money in a less than thoughtful manner.

. . .

You might feel as though your financial status, whether you're living in poverty or lower-middle class, is not entirely your fault. That's certainly true, however, we have to take responsibility for some of the spending habits in our life and take back control.

When we are spending our money without thinking, it can become a habit. The sooner you can start to implement better spending habits, the easier it will be to start saving money.

When you don't spend wisely and you know you're doing it, you will start to come up with justifications for those purchases. We likely have all experienced buyer's remorse in our lives.

We are changing the way our brain works when we consistently give in to poor habits, so it's time that we focus on what's important in life and to alter our thinking patterns in a positive way.

You might have heard the term discipline equals freedom most famously quoted by Jocko Willink, this applies to finances just as much as it applies to other parts of life.

. . .

THE LONG-TERM CONSEQUENCES of these financial habits can lead to having less access to top medical treatments and preventions. Worse nutrition if you cannot access the food needed to stay healthy. A stress level that is elevated and ruins many aspects of your life, and some say leads to chronic illnesses. Your access to romantic partners may diminish if you can't provide a stable environment or keep up with your competition in the dating marketplace. You will just have less options in all aspects of your life and your family will have less as a consequence.

IF YOU WANT your life to change, you must change. – Jim Rohn

THE BIG EXPENSES

Rent, cars, kids, college, and food are the biggest expenses most people struggle with, and it is understandable as to why it is this way. They are made at great expense, manufactured by experts, and do great things. We have safe building's, transport solutions, places of higher learning, access to the most educated people in our society, and food from every corner of the globe.

If we become highly focused and concentrate on lowering the costs of the main expenses, we can have a big impact on our cost of living, and change our future circumstances.

. . .

YOUR FIRST ACTIONS towards driving your costs down should be on your biggest expense, whatever that may be. We all have different things that we spend our money on, so not everyone's biggest expense is going to be the same.

WRITE out all your expenses and list them from top to bottom with the biggest expense at the top. For most, this will be their rent or mortgage, then maybe food, a car payment, and other loans/bills.

TRY to average out how much you are spending on things like entertainment, eating out, and so on. Each month might be different, so you don't need to really get into the details. Try to estimate how much might be spent on things like this.

DO this by adding up the last six months total expenses in each category, then divide it by 6, to get your average spend.

YOUR JOB IS to work through this the best you can from top to bottom with the help of this book, and any other resources you can find to help you eliminate your costs.

. . .

Over time, new technologies, techniques, and ideas will be available to all of us. So always keep your list to go over, and see if you can find new and innovative ways of cutting costs.

A great success principle to always remember is, what gets measured, gets accomplished!

Even after you have started your plan to save money, continue to evaluate these expenses. You might change what you spend your money on, and if you want to continue down the path of success, you should aim to consistently analyse your financial information.

Try to beat your record for each category each month and make a game out of saving. Make sure your total expense goes down every month, and try not to create many new expenses with the profits.

It's hard to relax and enjoy yourself with your family and friends when thinking about debts, taxes and rents.

. . .

Confucius put it best over 2500 years ago, not long after the first known currencies were created in 600 B.C.

"He who will not economize will have to agonize" – Confucius

RENT A KILL

The biggest expense for most people, in modern society, is rent, especially in the big cities around the world. London, New York, San Francisco, and Hong Kong have rents in the $2,000 to $3,500 range, on average.

The average person in these cities does not have jobs paying any more than they would be able to earn in another smaller cheaper location. The salaries might be higher in Chicago than a small town in Illinois, but the cost of living will far exceed that difference.

So many people are living on minimum wage, and doing so while living in the big cities. I don't know how or why they stay, maybe family commitments or the perks of living in this particular location, but it can't be anything more than a constant uphill battle.

SOME PEOPLE WORK FROM HOME, on the internet, and still choose to live and struggle in the big cities. There are certainly benefits to these cities, but it's more than just the rent that is higher. You can go to a small bar in Kentucky and get a beer for $2, but that same brand of beer might be $8 in a NYC bar. Sales tax can be higher as well. The location can drive up the price of everything, not just utilities.

YOU KNOW where I am going with this, and for some of you, this will be painful. You will be better off long term trying to relocate to a different city, maybe even a different country. Whether you're capable of moving to the suburbs, the countryside, or moving abroad, it can make a huge difference in your financial status.

YOU MIGHT NOT ENJOY LIVING SOMEWHERE that isn't as exciting as the city, but you will be able to save more money that can be used to travel frequently.

Why live in one expensive city scraping by, when you can live somewhere cheap and travel to different cities and countries several times throughout the year?

I'M GOING to use the United Kingdom as an example. Renting a studio flat in central London costs upwards of $1800. If you drive an hour outside of the city, a studio flat will cost you $900. If you are willing to drive another hour, you will find studio apartments for just $500. The cheapest studio apartments in England rent for $260.

IF YOU ARE willing to emigrate, and have the skills to work anywhere, or you can work online, the options available to you are quite unbelievable. You can even consider selling your things and move from place to place and live throughout the world in different furnished apartments.

IN ANTALYA TURKEY the average rent is just $200. In Braga Portugal, the average is $350. In Sofia in Bulgaria it's $400. Athens Greece, Phuket Thailand, Bucharest Romania, and Granada in Spain all rent at an average of $450.

. . .

I don't know what you are paying for rent. I am sure you can find a way to save something by moving to a cheaper location that suits your lifestyle. Your living situation never has to be permanent either. Maybe you could consider living in a cheaper area for a year while you save enough to get yourself back on your feet.

You will probably find somewhere you can have a higher standard of living for a lot less money. Not only is it a good idea for you to consider living somewhere else, but if you are an entrepreneur, it can be easier to start a business somewhere cheaper as well. You might think that opening a store in the heart of L.A. would bring the most traffic, but you could also lose your money faster in these high rental areas. You could try a smaller town instead, starting small can give you the solid foundation you need to expand further later on.

There are lists of world average rental prices to look at, so you can find locations that you will be comfortable with, and even excited about. If you can't, or won't, move, there are ways to make money and cut costs from where you live now.

. . .

THE FIRST WAY TO make money is by renting out extra rooms in your home or apartment., It is even worth considering turning the front room into another bedroom for this purpose. Even someone with a 1 bed flat can rent out the front room as a bedroom.

IF YOU HAVE ENOUGH BEDROOMS, it could possibly cover your entire rent or mortgage payment. This takes away a massive amount of financial pressure for many people living in the world's capitals.

ALWAYS GET permission from the landlord if you are renting out rooms in a rental property. Rent out rooms by the night using Airbnb and other service providers so you can run your rooms like a self-service hotel. Give your guests added perks as well, like cooking them breakfast, giving them access to toiletries, and so on.

YOU CAN MAKE MORE money using this strategy than renting the rooms long term, but you might not fill all the rooms every month. Test to see how many rooms you can fill for a couple of months, then fill the rest of the rooms with long term tenants, to maximize your profitability. There are lots of tutorials and courses online explaining how to do this.

ANOTHER OPTION for free accommodation is becoming a house sitter. You can do this long or short term. It sometimes involves looking after pets. You can hop from house to house to sit animals and watch homes, never having to pay rent, but also making money from the homeowners.

MAKE sure that you are always respectful and only do this if you plan on being the only one living in the house. If you abuse your privileges while housesitting, you can end up being out of a home and a job.

JUST SIGN up to one of the house-sitting sites available and you're ready to get started. Some long stays are for over a year. Some people have really nice houses for you to house sit, and it's free.

IF YOU HAVE a parking space you are not using, you can rent this out to people who work in the surrounding area. You can find people who might like to rent your parking space by going to the surrounding offices and leaving them an offer and your details. You could use a service like JustPark, who rent out your space and charge you a small fee.

It is better to get a long-term parking agreement, as it is less hassle. You might make more money renting by the hour or day like many do in big cities.

If you live next to a company that has clients coming and going but does not have parking, you might get a few people parking each day. Let the manager know so he can remind his customers that you have a space available. It's a win-win-win situation for you, the manager, and their customers.

There are also alternative types of accommodation to consider outside of houses and flats. You can live on a narrow boat with a mooring in most cities for way less than renting a flat. You can even buy your own boat and find the perfect spot to live.

If you are not comfortable driving the boat, you can always hire someone to move it for you. You can find boats that need to be renovated to save money. They tend to be cheaper when not moored in a big city, so buy outside the city and just drive to where you want to live.

Caravans and RVs are a great way to have cheap housing, with the added advantage of changing the place you live whenever you want, and being able to travel easily. With this option, you can find a price point that's right for you and make the best of what you can afford.

A clever way to take advantage of Caravans and RVs is renting them out from people that have vehicles parked for most of the year. Some caravan parks let you stay most of the year, some don't, but it's worth checking before committing to a contract.

If you are desperate, and you cannot find any of the options above, you can try things like warehouses with living facilities or empty business premises. You can ask the landlord to rent to you while he keeps looking for a business tenant.

. . .

Is there a need for property guardians in your area? Property guardians are needed to look after empty homes and help owners of these properties keep their property safe from squatters and vandalism.

Different types of arrangements can be made between the owner and the new occupier. Some arrangements require occupants to give a certain number of hours volunteering with charitable organizations, and some are paid arrangements, but some are free for the price of being a guardian.

Look online for property guardian programs in your area, or a place you are interested in living.

Again, these things can be temporary. It can be hard to switch from lease to lease in some apartments because you might need to have the first month's rent money, renter's fee, deposits, or move-in fees when finding a new place.

For the truly hardcore saver you could live in your car, you can ask friends to shower at their place, or use a gym like the y.m.c.a or use public shower facilities if they are available. When it comes to cooking, ask friends if you can use their kitchens by repaying them with a free home-cooked meal. Again, situations like these can be temporary and just a way to save up money for a month or two.

Cost of Living ***Geography Lesson***

It is amazing how a small change in location can have a massive effect on your cost of living. New York is one of the most expensive places to live. You could move to Ontario Canada where it's estimated to be 43% cheaper than New York and housing is estimated to be 60% cheaper.

Another example is London, it is 35% more expensive in London than living in Manchester, and 39% more expensive than Liverpool. The housing in Liverpool is 49% cheaper than in London.

If you are willing to go further, you can save even more by starting again in another country. It's cheaper to live in Barcelona in Spain, Porto in Portugal, and Athens in Greece than to live in Detroit, Michigan in the United States.

. . .

The cheapest city in the world, is Antalya in Turkey. I have been there and it's beautiful. It's a very popular holiday destination and is located on the Mediterranean coast. It costs 71% less to live in Antalya than in California. Turkey is a predominantly Muslim country so that might be a culture shock for some that are not well traveled.

The most expensive city to live in is Hamilton in Bermuda, a British Island Territory found east of Florida. It costs 46% more to live there than in Miami Florida.

You can have a look at where your city and country rank on sites like expatistan.com and compare it to places you have dreamed to see or live in.

Some people really should just move to a place with a better standard of living, in a safer environment, at a lower cost of living. If anything can change your life for the better, it's a change of environment.

. . .

WHERE WOULD YOU GO? How far are you willing to go? Are your skills needed in this country? Can you work online? If you go somewhere 50% cheaper you can maintain the same standard of living and take the rest of the month off. If time to do the things you want is more important to you than having excess savings to play with, you can make this happen by living somewhere 50% cheaper.

LOOK into the quality of living index by M*ercer* to get an idea of what people think about living in their city.

A GOOD EXAMPLE of moving to a city with a higher quality score and saving money is moving from New York City to Dusseldorf Germany. Dusseldorf is 37% cheaper and ranks at number 6 in quality score, whereas New York ranks at number 44.

SOME OF THE quality score factors might not be as important to you as they are to someone else. Don't just rely on the quality score to make your decision. It is still worth looking at, just to get an idea of all the accumulated services like healthcare, schools, transport, etc.

. . .

If you're living in a terrible area full of violence and stress, nothing is stopping you from moving somewhere else. Even moving just, a couple of hours away can have a dramatic effect on your life. Find a way to get some money together and make the move.

If you're living on low wages and working for a large company, try and get a transfer to one of the company's other locations where living is cheaper. This is a great way to try and get a promotion as well. Your store location might not give you much opportunity to advance, but maybe another location needs a team leader, manager, or supervisor. In this scenario not only would cost of living be cheaper, but you'd also be able to make more money now or in the future.

If you're renting, you only have to wait until the end of the contract before moving somewhere else. If you have a house with a mortgage, don't feel stuck. Get yourself a letting agent and have the house rented out for you while you're living somewhere else.

. . .

Even just doing the exercise of looking at all the destination options available to you, can set in motion something great in your future. Some cities and towns have great incentive programs to get you into their citizenship, here are a few of my favourites.

Alaska offers a permanent fund to its citizens made up out of their oil dividends. The dividend paid to all citizens for 2019 was $1,100 in a year of low oil prices.

If you love Italy, Candela is offering $2,350 just to move there.

If you hold a Swiss passport maybe consider Albinen, an Alpine village offering $25,300 for every adult and $10,000 for every child who moves there. You have to commit to living there for 10 years.

Harmony, Minnesota offers $12,000 to people who want to build their own homes and live in it.

. . .

New Haven, Connecticut gives out $80,000 in incentives, including a $10,000 interest-free loan towards a deposit on a home. That loan is forgivable after 5 years. Anyone working in public services receives an extra $2,500 towards a deposit. They offer new residents $30,000 for a renovation on this home and $40,000 towards certain educational programs.

Ponga in Spain offers young couples $3000 for becoming a citizen and $3000 more for every child they bring. Then $3000 more for every child that is born there. Amazing!

Look out for different and new incentives that become available, especially if you're moving to another town. They might not bother telling you about the incentives.

Many people looking for cost reduction by moving abroad look to southeast Asia. Malaysia, Thailand, and India have some great places to live long term and your savings will go far in these countries.

. . .

It can be scary to move somewhere new that you've never spent any extended period of time in, but it can be even scarier to live your life without having any financial security.

Who knows who you might meet, the things you might see, and the opportunities that will arise if you decide to take a chance and live somewhere new?

HOMEOWNER HACKS

If you own your own home with a mortgage or without one, there are lots of different options to consider. They can make you money, lower your expenses, and add to the quality of your life.

Downsize without moving and stay in your home. You can do this by splitting the house you own into smaller houses or flats. You can do this with an average sized terraced house and make the upstairs a flat to rent.

If your local council agrees to let you split the titles of your home into 2, you can sell the upstairs. If the council does not let you do this, you can still make up-stairs into a separate dwelling that you rent out to tenants. Check your local laws, but no one can stop you from renting out bedrooms to long term tenants.

If you're considering selling your property, remember to renovate and show it to the best of your ability, and add value in any way you can. Presentation matters when selling and some things add more value than others. Do not expect people who are viewing your home to see the potential. It's like most things in life, it is getting judged on face value.

Bedrooms beat almost everything else when it comes to adding value in most highly populated areas. A basement with a tiny window, that's a bedroom. So, get that room renovated, the same goes for the loft space. Check out how much other houses near you are selling for online with these benefits, then get some quotes for the work and do the math.

You can always try and rent out the upstairs as a holiday let or a serviced accommodation property as well. Again, check your laws, as things are always changing.

Renting out rooms for long term or serviced accommodation can be a great addition to any home with an empty room. I would sleep on the living room sofa to rent out my bedroom if I was in debt.

If you are struggling with your repayments or they are adding un-needed stress to your life, consider switching to a fixed interest only mortgage. Or try extending your mortgage back up to the maximum amount of years the lender will offer you.

It is always cheaper to switch your plan with your mortgage provider at the end of your initial period. It is usually cheaper to move to another company to find a better rate. Use a comparison site or two, and find a great offer.

Bland Designs, Renovation at Low Cost

. . .

As soon as you think, "how much will it cost to cosmetically refurbish my home," a second job, and the thought of selling your kidney to a billionaire start to sound like sensible ideas.

No need to worry, cosmetic and light refurbishment doesn't need to cost an arm and a leg, not even a kidney.

The most expensive rooms to renovate are the kitchen and bathrooms in most cases. Things like basement and loft conversions cost more, but we will not cover those today.

Let's start with the Kitchen. For some, it's the focal point of the whole house where people come together, talk, eat and share time with each other.

Here are a few ways to revive those cabinets and worktops, even if they are laminate. One of the most common ways to revive cabinets, especially wooden cabinets, is to just paint them with cupboard paint and add new handles. Some people like using chalk paint but it's not always the best.

. . .

If you have laminate cupboards you can do the same using laminate paint and smooth rollers. I find it's best to take the doors off the hinges and sit each door on top of a box to roll and then leave to dry.

Another way to revive your kitchen is to have it wrapped. It's like having your car wrapped but works just as well for your kitchen. It is surprisingly cheap and you might even want to try doing it yourself. Practice on one door first.

There are companies that sell doors rather than whole kitchens, which is more expensive than the options above but cheaper than buying a whole new kitchen.

Countertops can be wrapped, or you can get different types of overlays made of quartz and other materials.

Change the handles with other handles that have the same fitting, just unscrew and screw them back together.

. . .

You can buy kick boards and side panels separately as well.

If you just have to have a new kitchen, look on Facebook marketplace, Gumtree, Craigslist, and eBay for free and cheap kitchens. Many people are giving you the old kitchen, for the inconvenience of getting rid of theirs.

Bathrooms can be expensive. The bathroom suite is usually much cheaper when bought as a package with everything included.

If the color of the bath or sink does not match or they are just damaged or discoloured, you can use an enamel kit to paint it back to as good as new. You will want to do this if you have an especially expensive bathtub you want to keep.

Shop around and look for secondhand suites to find a bargain. Look for bargains from multiple stores on tiles. You might be surprised how much of a discount you will find. eBay usually has lots of tiles at cheap prices, but you usually have to pick them up from the owner's house.

. . .

Walls, ceilings, wood and radiators, it's just filling sanding and painting all the way around from top to bottom. Anyone can do it with the help of a few YouTube videos.

There are a few flooring options as well. Carpets can be brought back to life with a steam cleaner. If you think the carpet looks tired, why not try this before buying a new one.

If your floorboards are ok, why not sand and varnish, or even paint them, rather than covering them up, it's cheaper and looks better. You can do this yourself if you have the confidence to try.

The more skilled you are the more money you can save at home, so get learning.

You can even have your exterior doors and windows wrapped and save yourself a small fortune not changing them.

. . .

GET creative and look into all the ways people use ordinary materials to liven up their living space.

IF YOU PLAN AHEAD and create a list of materials from your chosen vendors you will not be so tempted to buy everything in one place while you're at the local hardware store for double the price. Happy Renovating.

FURNITURE FINDER

THIS SECTION IS GOING to cover how to furnish your home for less and still have a stylish home.

IT'S TIME TO SEARCH, collect, fix, up-cycle, mix and match with paint and stain. That's the game.

LET'S start with where to find quality pieces of furniture for free or cheap. The first place to look is on the free sites like Gumtree's free section or another free stuff site. Look through Facebook Market and eBay for tons of products not getting any bids because no one wants to pick them up. You might need to hire a van or pickup truck to take advantage of all these great offers. Having a car or a pick-up truck is always helpful and worth considering for business and money savings purposes.

Another great place to look for furniture is in charity shops, especially large chain store charity shops that have warehouses full of furniture. You can stain or paint the furniture to bring it up to modern standards and make all your furniture matches.

You can make some furniture and ornamental type objects yourself on YouTube, but you are better off looking for free products to save time. Unless you feel like making something for the fun out of it.

THE TRANSPORTER

Transport is usually one of the top expenses, especially when you consider families with multiple cars sitting in the driveway. Transportation industries are all about making money as well, so if you really want to save your cash, then it's time to re-evaluate the way that you get around.

A car can be a status symbol, the key to freedom, a hobby, but it can also be a financial mistake. Let's try and make sure your car is a gift and not a curse.

There are a ton of things you can do in order to save money in this department, but firstly, let us discuss what not to do.

. . .

Do not buy a new car off the lot when you can buy a used car with low mileage in the same condition for 3 quarters of the price. Most of the time, you can find cheaper used cars by looking on sites like auto trader.

Do not buy a car with low miles per gallon if you can't afford to refill all the time. Your lifestyle might change and you might need to take long journeys consistently, which puts you at the gas station spending your hard-earned cash on petrol or diesel rather than something of value. If you buy a car with half the miles per gallon of the car you own, you save 50% on your petrol bill every year.

Do not buy a car that's just too expensive for you, just to feel like you fit in. You might look cool now, but in a few years, that car will be outdated and you'll be stuck with a high payment for something that has lost its value, and its wow factor.

Do not get a lease car for a price based on using low mileage. You might come to realize you need to drive way more, and your lease company increases your monthly payments beyond what is affordable. Work changes, school changes and hospital visits can change your mileage beyond the deal offered by the lease company.

Let's discuss what you can do instead if you have to buy a new car. Look for models of cars that lose their value rapidly and take advantage by buying one of these bargains to make thousands in savings over the coming years.

Pay for your low-priced car in full, if you have some savings.

Financing is only good if you are going to be putting the remaining capital you have towards financial investments.

Low emissions can help you get lower tax and insurance bonuses in some countries. It's worth looking into these before you make a purchase.

Mopeds and Motorbikes can be cheap but dangerous. I don't recommend. These might be cheaper, but if you live somewhere that experiences harsh winters, then you won't be able to drive them safely during this time anyway.

Alternative transport should always be considered when trying to save money. Cycling is good if you live somewhere that it's safe to cycle, and not too far from where you need to work and study. It costs nothing after purchasing. You will also find that it helps increase your overall health.

Public transport, if the services where you live are reliable and fairly priced, can be an amazing alternative to purchasing a car. If you are retired, you can get public transport free in many countries. Always discuss with employers while job hunting if they offer transport compensation as well. You can also ask your current bosses for days that you might be able to work from home in order to save some money.

Share a car, or cars, between the family and use other services when needed. Between using a bicycle, public transport, and using services like Uber and cabs, you should be able to save some money. Though I would suggest only using Uber or Cabs in emergency as they can be pretty expensive.

. . .

If you're a family of 3, you will be paying 3 lots of car tax, 3 lots of insurance, petrol, MOT, services, repairs, and possibly payments towards purchasing the vehicles. It can add up to thousands of dollars leaving the household every month.

If you can choose to work from home and swap in the car for a bicycle, you're doing your family a favor and getting some exercise at the same time.

In 2017 the average car ownership cost per year was $8,469. Let's times that by 3 for our family setting, and costs work out to $25,407 for the average American family. Do you think it's worth reassessing the need for this major expense? Try to see if your family can attempt a slimmed down version of its transport needs and save over 100k every 4 years.

A lot of different types of services are going to be available soon, and car ownership will drop, as subscription-based services will become more viable.

. . .

You can use car-pooling apps already for long and short distances. This can save you a lot of money. You can take advantage of either making money from picking people up, or saving money by using other people in your area's passenger seat for a small fee.

There are already some car subscription services available with pick up and drop off locations. There are some services where you can just abandon the car within a certain radius.

A world of subscription-based cars is just around the corner. Some car companies are looking to offer self-driving cars. They will drive themselves to your destination, pick you up, wait for you or go back to the company car park. These cars will most likely be all electric so will be low cost for the companies to run and the subscription prices will most likely reflect that.

Walking and Other Foot Travel

. . .

If you have two feet and two legs that work properly and have no other health conditions holding you back, then you should start to use those limbs to move your body! Our legs are the biggest forms of free transportation we have at our disposal.

If you work five miles away, it's crazy to assume that you're going to walk to and from work every day. However, maybe there is an alternate route you can discover which will help you to save some money. For example, maybe at the present moment you take two different busses to and from work every day, resulting in a higher fare.

What if you could walk half a mile to a different bus stop, and then get dropped off a little further from where you're used to? Maybe you can find one single bus to take you to work so that you don't have to pay two different fares.

Alternatively, look at how you park. Do you park in an expensive parking garage right next to your work? Can you park a little farther for cheaper and make up the distance with walking?

. . .

We often think of transportation in an "all or nothing," kind of mentality. You either have to drive all the way or walk all the way. Don't think like this. Look for ways you can combine both.

Even if you do live far from work, maybe you could have one day that you walk home instead of taking the bus or a cab. For example, maybe Friday after work you walk home. Even if it takes you an hour, you can count that as your workout for the day. You can beat the rush hour traffic and get a nice exercise in before going home, showering, and getting ready for the weekend!

Could you get a ride from a co-worker and get a ride from them each day?

You would want to help them out with gas or you could pay them in the form of a coffee or occasional breakfast rather than filling up their gas tank. You could cut down on your commute by simply combining walking with carpooling.

. . .

If none of these work for you, and you simply hate walking, or think it's not fast enough, remember the other ways that you can use your feet!

Bicycles, roller blades and scooters can be hard to learn, but they can also offer you some added methods of travel that won't require as much work as walking. It will be hard to get going, but once you have learned how to use these things, you can cut down your commute time.

These can be more physically demanding at first, but once you've gotten used to them, they can offer a quicker more exciting way to commute than walking, and they'll be a lot cheaper as well.

Added Benefits of Cutting Transportation Costs

If you don't live in a big city with public transportation, or if you just come from somewhere more rural and driving is the only option, you can still save money. One way to do this could be in the form of using your car for money as well.

. . .

THERE ARE SO many ride share apps that you could sign up for which could help you make more money. This could become a second part-time job to help you make your car payments. You don't have to work at this all the time. You can simply come up with the amount needed to pay your car payment, insurance, and gas. Just take enough rides to cover these costs.

USE THE CAR, that costs you money, to make money or at least pay for itself.

ALTERNATIVELY, you could see if there was a way to use your car to make money to and from work. If you have to leave for work at 9 am every morning to make it in by 10 am, then why not wake up one hour earlier and use those hours to drive other people to and from their jobs. As long as you pick rides in the direction of where you need to go, you can still make it to work on time.

YOU SHOULD ALSO CONSIDER how you can reduce your car insurance and overall car payments. Always check for the option to refinance your loans when possible. At the same time, make sure that your car insurance is the lowest it can possibly be. If you are a consistently good driver with a good amount of no claim's discounts, you can even find places that offer extra rewards for good drivers.

FOOD DOUGH

Imagine cutting your food bill by a third just by growing food in your garden. It's possible for you to do this if you're willing to put in the work.

We all have to eat. It can be a pleasure, a way to get together, something we look forward too, and it can cost a lot of money. Unfortunately we have to take notice of our grocery bills.

If you are in an area where you can forage for food, hunt, and fish with the right permissions, it makes things even easier. That option is not available to most people living in cities and towns where the majority of the human population now lives.

. . .

If you have a garden why not get yourself some chickens and have free eggs all year, this is probably the cheapest way to acquire high-quality protein for your family, without the need to hunt. You can even sell the excess eggs each week by leaving an honesty box to take payment in your front yard next to the basket of eggs. You can use an honesty box for all types of products, but expect the occasional theft to occur, expect it so you don't get too upset about it.

The average monthly cost of food in the U.S. is $550. You could at least half that by growing your food and making some simple choices. You should be able to get it down to $275 or less.

Gardening

Your garden can save you money and make you money in many ways, for a small investment and a few hours a week. Here are some good examples: valentines' roses, fruit, vegetables, chickens and eggs, salad mix, sunflower, pea shoots, arugula, spinach,

Hakurei, mushrooms in the shed, potatoes, bees and honey.

If you live in the Mediterranean, landscaping trees and shrubs, Japanese maples, bonsai trees, willows, bamboo, gourmet garlic, elephant garlic. Garlic is known as the mortgage lifter and are hardy plants. Saffron is labor intensive but makes sense for some people, especially in the long term as it's the world's most expensive spice.

If you haven't got an outdoor garden look into indoor gardens and all the ways people are growing their food. Spinach, lettuce, mushrooms, arugula, and potatoes work well.

If you only have a small garden, you can still save money by growing your food. You never have to worry about not being able to provide food for your family.

If you have a large garden, you could potentially make enough money to cover your yearly food bill, if you have a few acres maybe the rental as well.

Fasting, Rice, Noodles, Water

Another way to decrease your spending is just by eating less and fasting for one meal a day. For some people, this will seem a little extreme but the health benefits of fasting are widely known, and for most full-grown people it's fine. I would consult a doctor and would let the children get a pass on the fasting method.

If you fast just one meal a day, you decrease your monthly spend by a third just using this method. That is at least an extra thousand dollars a year for most people.

Food choices make a massive difference. If you live on take out you are throwing your money away. You are also missing out on being able to create your own, made to personal taste, meals.

Soups, rice, noodles, pasta, and other cheap products can be used to make up a lot of your meals. Add sauces, herbs, and spices, possibly grown from your own garden.

There are websites listing meals you can make for less than a dollar per serving. I recommend trying to add some of these into the list of meals you regularly eat. The average person eats 21 meals per week. If you can make your meals for a dollar, you will be paying less for a month's meals than most people are paying for a couple of take out dinners.

You can make meals for way less than a dollar, like soups, and spend next to nothing on a bowl of rice with some vegetables. So, it is possible to get your food bill down to a very small percentage of your weekly budget, if you are willing to change the way you eat.

Another cost that adds up is bottled water. You can filter your water at home and put it into glass pitchers, add fruit to it for flavor, and enjoy something that should naturally be free. You can make your tea and coffee at home as well.

. . .

If possible, take packed lunches when you have to be away from home, working and studying.

Ok let's recap. Grow food, get chickens, fast one meal, make meals for less than a dollar, and don't pay for water or expensive coffee. These things should be obvious to all of us, but we fall into the patterns of the people around us. We participate in social norms, rather than thinking about what is in our own best interest.

Food is growing out of the floor, water is in our taps, and you get 10 servings of rice for 70 cents. Reasonable, healthy food is cheap, but our decisions are expensive.

Other Meal Replacements

Buying multiple ingredients for one meal can be complicated and expensive.

. . .

If you are someone that doesn't cook often, you might purchase separate things based on their ingredients.

We all deserve to have enjoyable meals, but when every meal we make from home has to have 100 different elements, it can lead to spiralling costs and throwing away a lot of food that goes out of date.

Look for ways that you can reduce, not just how much you spend when shopping, but how many individual items you buy, which leads to waste.

Consider adding smoothies to your diet. If you just replace one meal a day with smoothies, then you might find that it's easier to cut down on how much you're spending on individual ingredients. Many of the things that would have been thrown out can be used in your smoothies and this also cuts down on waste.

You'd never think to eat berries, spinach, and milk separately as a meal. That's boring! You can blend them together, however, and you will have a healthy meal full of flavor that will keep you full for hours.

. . .

This is a great way to reuse veggies and fruits that might be go bad otherwise.

You can freeze your smoothies in ice cube trays. When it comes time to eat them, pop them out and blend them with some milk or water so that they're creamy once again. This is something that many health enthusiasts already do, not just because it's cheap, but because it's good for you!

Smoothies aren't everyone's cup of tea, but there are still ways that you can reduce the amount of food that you're buying by cutting down on wastage.

When you go out to eat, try and cut what you're getting in half to make it last for two meals. You will start to realize that you can still eat out, and just stretch it for two meals rather than just spending your budget on one.

There are a ton of ways that you can increase your meal without paying extra for it as well. Of course, I would encourage you to never eat out to save your money, but that's not always realistic. Students and workers who have to eat in between work breaks and classes need to eat and that usually makes fast food the easiest and sometimes the only option, if you can make the time in the mornings to make your food at home this can be much cheaper than being at the mercy of the restaurants and cafeterias. We often go on dates over meals, and they can be a great way to socialize and hangout with other friends.

Before going to your restaurant of choice, always look up first to see if there are any "hacks" that will help get you a bigger meal that you could stretch into two servings. Look for the current deals available and get the best deal.

Grocery Shopping Experiments

What types of experiments can we run to find out how your particular family can enjoy lower shopping bills?

The first is the simplest, just switch supermarkets and see what happens. Every family uses different products so there is no easy answer to find the cheapest store for you.

. . .

HERE IS a list of stores to try. Take note of your total bill each time to compare to the other stores: Aldi, Lidl, Costco, Dollar Tree, Walmart, and Iceland are some of the cheaper store's worth adding to your first experiment.

ANOTHER EXPERIMENT TO try is looking to the international aisle for products with little known brands selling for cheaper prices. This might open up a whole new world of foods you have tried before and save you some money.

BULK BUY the basics by using wholesale stores like Costco to save on everyday items. If you don't have space but still want to benefit from this, you could pull together your friends and split the cost so everyone benefits.

IF YOU HAVE a loft or basement make use of this for buying things in bulk, a deep freezer is brilliant for this reason.

. . .

LOOK for frozen versions of refrigerated food so you don't throw out food when it goes past the expiry date.

IF YOU BUY a lot of cleaning products look into making your own. The ingredients that are used in these products like bicarbonate soda are so much cheaper when bought separately it is probably a hundred times cheaper. Instead of looking at the total price of an item, for example toilet paper, look at the per unit price. The lowest per unit price is what you want to purchase. You might spend a higher total, but you will be getting much more of that product.

THE COUPON DON

Cutting coupons can be hard, but it can also be a great way for you to save a ton of money. Every single store that you go to will have coupons. Make sure that you check online before going there. Aside from that, check out specific products that you can get a coupon for. Most of the time, generic brands will be cheaper, however, many name brands will offer coupons and generic brands frequently won't.

Before going shopping, always make a grocery list. Then, google search different brand names for the products that you want, to see if they have any coupons available. For example, let's say that you need to buy toilet paper. The generic brand would be the first option, but this can be rough and thin, so it's not the top choice. Google search the brands of products like toilet paper to see if anyone has any coupons. You might google "Charmin coupons," "Quilted Northern coupons," or "Angel soft coupons."

They won't always have coupons, but it's still worth checking out.

Always shop for clearance items. If you aren't sure what to make for a meal, go to the store and base your meal plans around what's on clearance. Make sure to check dates, as many things will be marked down before they expire.

Still, these also might be things you can freeze, pickle, or store in another way that elongates their life. This will also be a chance for you to really get creative with the things that you choose to make.

Find out when your store might be getting new shipments, and see if they put things on sale the day of or the day after.

. . .

When picking produce priced by weight, pick out the smallest ones possible to reduce wastage per meal.

An onion might only be $1 a pound, so it might not seem like a big difference. However, if you buy a big one, it could be $1.20. You could buy a small one for $.80, without even seeing that much of a size difference. We usually throw away a lot of the excess veggies anyway.

If you do this for ten different veggies in one grocery trip, you've saved a few dollars. This will add up throughout your different grocery trips, and could save you a lot over time.

SHARE, SWAP, TRADE, HELP, WORK

Saving money is not always about getting things for free or ridiculously cheap, it's about sharing amongst larger and larger groups. Swapping things with people and saving the pricing issue for other occasions. Helping someone get what they want, so you can get what you want and working for the benefits rather than just money.

Did your parents tell you it was good to share? They were right. Unfortunately, that is where it stopped and as we have grown up, instead of becoming better sharers, we have become worse sharers.

When you were young you had no choice but to share, you had to share one object with someone else. When we grow up, we try to get away from this by having everything for ourselves and not having to contend with anyone else. This can be good for a lot of things and we all want as much independence as we can have, but you may be missing out on so many cool opportunities.

The downside to owning everything yourself is firstly, the money to purchase everything, and second, the loss of space in your home.

Even more important than this is losing the skill of sharing throughout your life and relationships.

Share in ever-expanding circles to increase personal benefit. Start with the family where most of us still occasionally receive the benefit of sharing things we own. Then move on to friends. Maybe only lend something small at first to build up trust between you if you are not that close. Now it starts to get interesting. Beyond friends and family, you can share amongst the village, town, city and maybe even country.

. . .

There are community sharing programs being started in towns all over the world. They share tools, lawn mowers, and everything else you can think of. If you haven't got one in your town, maybe you can be the person to start one. A Facebook group is probably all you need. You could advertise this amongst your friends online, and in the other community groups, and get something going in little to no time.

If you think the sharing scheme has no value, think about this. A street with 1000 houses probably has 1000 lawn mowers, 1000 bicycles, 1000 spades and shovels, 300 sets of unused free weights, and 100 cars that have not moved in ten years.

It is crazy to think everyone in your neighbourhood could probably be better off just by pooling together some resources that they do not use.

Remember to go old school and trade things in return for what you want. The last time you did this was probably in school, for some stickers or playing cards. It's amazing that we seem to lose the will or creativity when we get older to do simple trades for the things we have. Use the skills or services we can offer as a trade. Perhaps even teach someone something as part of a trade.

Luckily, some sites on the internet have popped up to help us barter for different things. There are even sites that help you swap your house permanently with someone else, no estate agents needed and no mortgage brokers needed. Have a look into these bartering sites and see what other people are asking for, maybe you have it, and maybe they have what you want.

If you're good at up-cycling furniture, swap sites might be a great place for you to find something.

Similar to trading things, is taking advantage of 2 for 1 offers and splitting the cost, or taking turns who pays each time. There are lots of these offers, and people don't take advantage of them because they don't know to ask a friend about splitting the cost.

Help and work for people, businesses and other organizations for the perks of the job rather than the pay. You might want to meet like-minded people, travel and get paid for the pleasure, learn a skill, get fit, and many other perks that some organizations offer.

You can join the Merchant Navy or the Army and travel the world at a young age. You can do this without getting involved in the military, there are all sorts of programs where you can teach in other countries after taking a simple course. There is a multitude of other opportunities available to anyone who seeks them.

You can have some of the perks of the rich just for picking the right occupation or long-term career.

Would you like to have a yacht? Just work on one all year while getting paid and learning. Would you like to have a great car or work in a factory of the best cars in the world, with the team designing them? Work in some of the greatest venues in the world and know the inside track on how everything works? Night clubs, hotels, cruise liners, stadiums, theatres, universities, tv and film studios, the choice is yours, so go and find something that makes your life more exciting, even before the paycheque comes each month.

. . .

ACCESS CAN BE ALMOST as good as ownership in some situations, especially if the company you're working for is failing. You can still smile, and you still get paid, no matter how well the business is doing, while the actual owners are stressed to their limits.

TOURIST

In most cities there are lots of things to do for free, and a lot of the things that are free are surprisingly good, they are often better than the paid exhibits.

Many museums holding the most important items in humanity's history, art galleries displaying the most famous works and historic buildings offer free entry; nature reserves, parks, outdoor festivals, parades, carnivals, beaches, hiking trails, outdoor sports, surfing, skiing, and other activities can cost little or no money.

If you want to travel to another state, you can try one of the crowd surfing sites. You can get free accommodation on your adventures or stay in a tent in a safe place recommended by other hikers.

You could use a car-pooling app for the ride to town, or use a greyhound bus or train to your next destination.

Traveling within your own country when going for short stays is one of the cheapest ways to travel. If you're travelling for over a month, it can be cheaper to stay in a country that is cheaper than your own though, take advantage of cheap flights at certain times of the year, to places where living and travelling is cheaper than staying in your home country.

If you're hiking, it's acceptable to make up a tent on a trail. Why not do this and see the town or city as well? Benefit from having free accommodation while enjoying all the sights. Cooking your own food and making flasks of coffee and other drinks can cut your costs dramatically and save you loads of time queuing in restaurants.

If you are worried about having to walk around with a large bag, there are services like stasher who will look after your luggage and bags. They offer to keep your bags in hotels and stores for a small fee, leaving you to walk around, without that weight on your back. One bag a day costs $6 to stash and is insured up to $750.

Cycling touring across most countries with a tent ready to go is probably the cheapest way to travel. And the views you will wake up to some days will beat most hotels.

Folding bikes can be good for keeping in your car, camper, van, or boat.

If you can't cycle and want to use your car, you can even get a car tent to increase your indoor space and options.

I like the idea of the car, car tent, and foldable bike option.

Try to prepare yourself by doing your research and speaking to people online about the best places to stay, the safest journeys, and other tips to make a memorable adventure to treasure.

. . .

You can pick up a cheap solo tent like the Gelert Track 1 for under $50 to get started. I would recommend cooking your food on a stove. If there is a group of you, this will save you a ton of money and you can go in together to buy food.

In many major cities, you can spend your whole week visiting free attractions. Google free attractions and you should find plenty of things to do, it's probably best to do this before you decide on a location to visit.

Make sure to check out areas of natural beauty, its free and is probably going to be as good, or better, than a day in the city. In the US, if you are a student, have a child, or disabled, you can qualify for a free pass to all of the nation's natural parks.

House sitting is another brilliant way to travel, and live in free accommodation. It's worth trying, even if you only do it once.

. . .

Motorhome hire is super cheap and a great way to get accommodations and travel all in one. The site vroomvroomvroom.com is worth using when booking your motorhome, and so is Apollo.

If you are planning on flying to another country, consider looking at multiple airports to get the best price. And always travel to places offseason if you can. This will severely affect the prices and possibly save you hours in queues for attractions. Disney and The Roman Colosseum come to mind when thinking about queuing a long time for attractions.

If you are looking to do a cheap package holiday, try an all-inclusive package. If it gets good reviews, why not take advantage of non-stop food and drink.

If you're boating, try to take advantage of free moorings. There are apps available for finding them.

Travel cost for a big rail trip around Europe for 3 months is $1008 using the Eurail pass. It does not include accommodation, but you can pay to stay in a sleeper car on the night train.

. . .

The Amtrak pass would be the equivalent of the Eurail pass in the United States, offering 45 days of travel in 18 segments for $899.

Going Out, Friends and Family

Do you remember what life was like before high speed internet?

You used to see your friends a lot more, go out with them, and actually talk to them. Mobile phones were only used for talking and texting so people had all of your attention.

If you're one of the few people left who still likes to leave their internet cave and venture out into the world, this chapter might help you out.

Let's work through some of the things you can do with friends without spending your life savings.

You can group together these options for full, fun days out.:

- Go and visit your towns tourist attractions, it's kind of a shame not to. Many attractions are free or cheap. In the major cities there are free museums, galleries, aquariums, gardens etc.
- Organize board games, card games, and video game nights. In person with friends is still more fun than online gaming.
- Get a barbecue going or cook a meal together. Try cooking something from scratch and push your culinary skills to the next level.
- You know the parks you went to as kids are still there, right? Go play some sports, sit on the swings, and mess around for a while with your friends.
- Go hiking and get out in an environment that's natural. Explore and even go camping if you have the equipment and the time.
- Go fishing and foraging for fun and food.
- Have a picnic overlooking the water at the beach or the lake.
- Go surfing if you have a board. The waves are free.

- Make a scavenger hunt for your friends with a mystery prize for the winner.
- Get your bike out and go find some new places. Rollerblade around town or get the skateboard out.
- A safe bet everyone can get behind is a movie night or even a movie marathon weekend.
- Take a class with a friend. Polish up that embarrassing math, or learn a new language. A lot of towns offer free classes.
- Go for long walks and jogs just to explore new places and keep fit.
- Home workout with your friends. Use some space as a weights room or follow a fitness regimen on the tv.
- Go to a religious service, even if you're not religious. There aren't many places talking about morals and life, even if you don't feel that the church is correct in all its teachings, at least it is bringing up these types of subjects, and brings people together.
- Do some temp work, freelance work, or volunteer with a friend.
- The "bring your own everything party." Take some of the pressure off the host by making everyone bring everything they want.

- Go to the library, check out a book on something way out of your realm of experience. Open up new worlds to you through audio, video, and books.
- Try out the local book club and see how you like it.
- Do a yard sale with a friend. Sell your unwanted things, and make some money.
- Try the community theatre and try to spot the next great actor.
- Go to the farmers market and see what you can find.
- Visit the zoo, it's not free, but some zoos are big enough to take up a whole day.

If you save a $100 a week doing some of these activities, that's another $5,200 in your savings account each year.

Make sure to put multiple activities together to make some memorable days out.

~

Multi-Task Travels

. . .

TRAVELING IS an expense that we can easily cut from our lives as you don't have to travel to survive. However, if you always stay in the same place, it can be a lot less fun than exploring what the world has to offer. Understanding the world can pay off financially in the long term and open your eyes to so many opportunities that you didn't even know about.

SIGN up for rewards and go on trips where you will be receiving points and discounts if possible, to go towards your next adventures. If you have to have a credit card, which is highly discouraged, you need only take out one that offers travel perks. Stick to one airline that will give you more rewards the more you travel.

SOME PEOPLE WAIT until the last minute to go on a trip and see what flights might be cheapest. Last minute flight deals can be very cheap as the airline just wants to fill the last seat's they have available. This can help you discover interesting and new places you never would have gone to if you planned the trip earlier in advance.

. . .

If you freelance, look for gigs in other places every once in a while. If you write, shoot video, graphic design, or have any other creative talent, see if there are gigs for you to work while you're on a trip! Just take an extra day to stay after you've finished working the gig.

There is always going to be work and services needed in every country so don't be afraid to work abroad and let the work pay for your travelling. Maybe someone needs a house sitter or a dog watched, you can do this while on vacation.

Look for ways to not have to stay anywhere at all, Sleep on the plane and on the bus, travelling to the next destination at night and resting as you commute. Make sure to keep your belongings close.

SMART MONEY

If you are thinking about going to a University and furthering your education, really look into what the different colleges will offer. They can be amazing for networking with lots of people that will be able to help you in the future. If you get accepted to a top-ranking school, your opportunities are even greater, but remember, the cost will come with that too.

Scholarships, grants, and bursaries could be worth applying for, even though gaining these benefits can be a long shot.

. . .

IF THE PRICE for education in your country is high, why not try and apply to universities in other countries where education is FREE or cheap.

THE EUROPEAN INSTITUTIONS can be very good for this, have a look into Erasmus for more information.

WHAT YOU WANT, and how you achieve it are questions you probably don't want to deal with at a young age but you might as well take a shot at it.

SOME COURSES that offer no prospects for you are probably better served by just picking up all the literature on the subject yourself. Try using the library and listening to online lectures then the historical commentary on each book. Even using the open university and other online courses might provide insight at a similar level for free or a fraction of the price.

MIT HAS its online platform teaching many subjects including 2,400 courses, available for FREE.

. . .

Other free resources include YouTube, Khan Academy, Udemy, Coursera, Lynda, iTunes U, EdX, open Yale courses, BBC skills wise, the excellence gateway, and many other platforms.

Language apps and websites like Busuu, Duo Lingo, Memrise, Beelingua, hellotalk, and lingua lift are all mostly free. Hellotalk is a clever app where you send voice messages back and forth to people speaking other languages. Each app and website have their faults and merits but they are all worth trying out as they teach in different ways and focus on different aspects of learning and communication.

Some college courses are free. Math and English are usually the most likely to be free.

Pick courses that will pay off over the long term, the cost is only relevant to the return you make. Be hyper-focused on the skill and knowledge acquisition you intend to accumulate over the next few years.

. . .

If you need skills from a trade school to do the things you want, go to the trade school as well. If the skills are found online spend your time online.

Try to get a job in the field or start a business while still learning. All of these things are time restricted, but that is the same with everything. Find paid internships to help you continue to save money while gaining experience in your chosen field.

I recommend doing all these things at the same time, or whenever you possibly can. A lot of people get into a either or mentality when the option to have both is available. It's not that they aren't happy to have the choice, but choosing both can sound daunting. When both are available, you should do it, if that's what you want.

Ways to Cut Costs If You Have to Stay Off Campus

Rent out a house, then sub-let the rooms to other students. This should be discussed with the landlord, but not everyone does. You should cover your rental cost, and if you have enough rooms, make a profit.

You can use Airbnb to rent out rooms by the day if you can get the bookings.

If you can commute to the school, it's worth saving money this way. Unfortunately, it's not possible for most students at a university. Oftentimes, Universities require you to stay on campus for your Freshman year, but during that time you can be making arrangements with other students to rent a place together.

You can sign up to multiple libraries and lend the textbooks systematically for your course to avoid fines and save money buying the overly expensive text books.

Look for Kindle versions of the books you need. Get free public domain eBooks and sign up for kindle unlimited. Check to see if most of the books you want are available through the service providers.

If you buy the physical copies look for them second hand, as the price drops can be dramatic. You can also find them cheap by buying them from students just finishing the course. You can also do the same, selling the book when you are finished.

Learn to cook a bunch of cheap meals before going to college. You might find this will make you a whole lot of friends as well. You could even sell cheap meals to people in the dorms.

If you are looking for work while studying, why not sell your services on Fiverr or Upwork? You can do things like transcription and editing of other people's work to increase your income.

This type of work helps you increase the skills you are learning while at college. You will save time commuting to a brick and mortar business and free-lancing pays well for certain services.

Don't forget to have some fun and hopefully make some life-long friends. Do not underestimate the value of good friendships in this life.

Back to saving lots of money.

. . .

STUDENT DEBT IS a problem for millions of people and can make life difficult straight out of the gate. If you are paying a high-interest rate on your debt you can refinance the debt for a better rate and try to extend the terms for smaller repayments.

YOU WILL HAVE to do your research and get as much advice as you can before taking action. Every loan will have its terms and conditions, so the devil is in the details, be careful. When you leave college and get a job you might be able to get a personal loan with better terms than you have with your college.

IT'S hard to balance how much your education is worth. You can't see the untaken paths that would have unfolded.

JUST KNOW that trying to attain a better education is a good path rather than a bad one and you might not see the value in the experience until later in life.

I HOPE you try to balance your high paying skill acquisition against the size of the debt you have to take on.

DO I NOT ENTERTAIN!

If you have the internet, entertainment is free and more abundant than we ever thought could be possible. All the richest most powerful people that have ever lived, never had access to as much entertainment as us. The internet has changed everything.

IF YOU HAVE lots of cd's and vinyl collecting dust that you bought from Amazon, you are in luck. The Amazon auto-rip service gives you the digital versions free, giving you a new library of songs to listen to.

GAMING IS free if you want it to be. Some of the biggest games like League of Legends and Fortnite are free to play, along with thousands of others. This is a trend that will continue to grow as the free to play model has had some huge successes.

If you have to play on console, subscription services have arrived and will be on their way to most platforms. Xbox has led the way with the game pass service which offers a catalog of games for a small fee. Xbox also has a vast backward compatibility catalog that benefits anyone who owned a lot of games on the 360 or original Xbox. You can also find cheap used games on Craigslist, eBay, and Facebook Marketplace. This is a great place for you to sell your games as well. Try not to trade in to game stores, as you receive little compensation for your games. Always try to sell them yourself directly to the consumer first.

Google, PlayStation, Xbox, and Amazon have all taken an interest in creating cloud-based games that can be streamed as long as you have a subscription. I'm guessing Steam will try and replicate this for their catalog of pc games.

If you are struggling with your finances, satellite and cable have got to go. The streaming services like

Netflix and Hulu are way cheaper. If you want to lower your expenses, you can get rid of all your subscriptions and just use the free streaming services available online. YouTube, the most popular content platform in the world, and other free platforms worth trying are Sony crackle, Pluto tv, USTV NOW, BBC I player and Tubi Tv.

You can hop from free trial to free trial for the paid streaming services until you find your favorite. This can save months of subscription fees, and you will be sent some great offers from these companies to come back to them.

The number of free podcasts available on YouTube will keep you going forever. Try Joe Rogan, London Real, and Tim Ferris to watch some long-form conversations you just don't get to experience when watching TV.

YouTube has given lectures on every subject a place to call home, so you can educate yourself by listening to experts in every field from across the globe.

. . .

If you love books, most of history's best books are available for free in public domain libraries online. A good website to look at is the Gutenberg.org site offering over 57,000 books.

Some new books can be picked up on Amazon in their free section, this is where authors use a free promotion for their launch.

If you also like audio books, which are great to listen to while doing other things like driving, gardening or working out at the gym, you can find them on free podcasts. You can also subscribe to the audiobooks app which has thousands of free books. You can also get the amazon audible app and listen to lots of free shows by some excellent hosts like Steven Fry.

If you signed up to Amazon Prime, you might still not be aware of the Prime reading catalog you get for Free, offering loads of books and magazines. Prime also gives you Prime Video for free. They are rivaling Netflix, creating new shows by famous directors and writers like Neil Gaiman. They constantly update their free movies and you can purchase other movies to download for a fraction of the cost.

There are websites dedicated to free documentaries that have massive libraries that will educate you and possibly make a conspiracy theorist of you in no time. A site called top documentary films has a massive collection of free to watch documentaries.

So much entertainment for free!

Entertainment Outside of Media

Going to shows like concerts and stand-up comedy can be fun, but they can also be pricey depending on who you see. You don't have to give up on having a fun night life. Look for ways that you can enjoy these kinds of things without breaking the bank.

For starters, check out local bands that have free shows, or shows that have small suggested donations. You will start to discover bands that you might have never listened to otherwise.

. . .

You are also supporting your local artists, as well as smaller venues. The only price you will have to pay will be the amount for a drink or two while you enjoy these bands.

The same can be said for comedy shows as well. Go to open mic nights and listen to some of the smaller comedians in your area. The quality won't be as good as those that are selling out arenas of course, but you will still have the ability to get some laughs in. At an open mic night, most sets will only last a few minutes anyway. Sometimes watching them bomb or mess up could end up being funnier than the jokes they have as well.

You should also consider getting on social media to get free tickets to shows that you love. Always enter contests and do whatever you can to get discounts on some of the biggest names who might be coming to your area. At the same time, you can also Tweet at them or use Instagram DMs to try and get their attention. The chances of them seeing your requests are low, but it's still no cost to you to reach out. They might just end up putting you on the list or at least giving you a discount!

. . .

If none of this is something you want to try, you could consider trying to get work at these events. Not only will you get to see the show for free, but you can make money at the same time. Look at arenas or venues in your area that consistently have different kinds of big shows and concerts. See if you can get hired as security or a janitor. Most of the time these kinds of events over-hire people, meaning you won't have to do more than pick up some trash or stock the toilet paper. You will get a chance to get some views from exclusive seats, and you can even go home with a paycheque!

Many live concerts will be put online afterwards as well. You can search any big artist and then the city of their performance and find some sort of clip on YouTube. It's definitely not the same, but it can help alleviate some of those FOMO anxieties that might cause you to spend money you don't have.

SAVE YOUR ENERGY

Getting your energy bills down can be as simple as switching providers each year and changing a few little habits.

Obvious waste is the easiest place to start making savings. Having the lights on when it's sunny outside is a waste of electricity. Turning the heating on when you are barely clothed is a waste.

In Norway there is a saying, "there is no bad weather, only the wrong clothes". When you live in a mild climate you should rely on clothes more than your heating system.

A PROGRAMMABLE THERMOSTAT that has a decent app included should help you keep temperatures and bills at better levels.

IN COUNTRIES where it gets cold, you should make sure to seal everything and take precautions against cold spots from things like post boxes on your front door. You should try to insulate your home the best you can. Some governments have free insulation schemes for people. Some governments provide cavity wall insulation, loft insulation, and other technologies.

IF YOU ARE UPGRADING your windows consider the insulating effects of what you are buying. For a minimal upgrade in the price, you might get something that saves you a lot of money in the long run. Be careful though, windows and doors can be expensive and you should shop around to find the best deal, don't be afraid to negotiate a better price.

~

TRY to do all your battery charging at off-peak times for savings. Laptops, phones, and cars can be charged for less if timed correctly.

. . .

Don't forget to put all your electronics on the power saving mode available on all modern devices, including your television.

To turn off all your electrics at the plug easily, get a smart plug. Amazon has one that connects to Alexa through Wi-Fi. Turning off your plugs when not using saves you money because some appliances still receive electricity when they are not turned on, especially older appliances.

Your dust can make these appliances work less efficiently, so try to dust out all electronic products, so they can run the way they were intended to when purchased.

When buying new appliances check the energy rating so you don't increase your energy bill. Most new products will be substantially better energy-wise, than products that are 10 years old. Everything from your light bulbs to your laptop, have improved in efficiency. Almost all electronics have.

Using water is cheap, but it does add up to a nice bill sometimes.

. . .

THE MOST EXPENSIVE water is in the kettle, especially in England where drinking tea all day is the norm. A simple trick to cut down on the cost of this is keeping all the excess hot water in a thermos flask to make the next drink. This can be used for coffee and every other hot drink.

A COLD SHOWER cuts down on electric. I can't stand the cold showers so I'll happily pay. However, a cold shower can also help to wake you up in the morning, and cause you to want to take a shorter shower. There have been several studies conducted that link cold water, showers and baths, to a healthy cardio-vascular system, but I don't care.

A GOOD WAY TO cut down on wasting water when cleaning is using wash cloths. The amount of water needed to wash is tiny in comparison to a bath or a shower. Just wet the cloth add some soap, clean yourself then rinse off with another cloth, or quickly use the shower head.

SAVE rainwater in containers to feed your plants instead of using the hose every time.

. . .

Eco toilets, showers, and taps can help you save water. They cost a little bit more, but it is still worth considering the next time you fix or upgrade your bathroom or kitchen products.

Most people are better off with a water meter rather than estimated billing, but do some research into your area to see if this is correct. The size of your home usually plays a part and the number of people in the house.

Ok, back to energy savings.

If your house has wind and solar power, all your electricity needs could be free. The solar and wind pay you when you have an excess of power that gets sent back to the grid. The modern installations have greater energy efficiency that makes use of battery storage and software. The software makes sure you buy cheap electric if any is needed, by taking energy peak times into consideration.

. . .

Some countries offer free solar or incentives to purchase and many other schemes to help fight carbon emissions. Make sure to look into the fine print of these contracts, new companies are offering better deals every year. If you are replacing your roofing, look into solar roof tiles which could cost even less than traditional tiles.

If you don't have solar or wind power, a combi boiler is usually the cheapest way to get your energy. A gas cooker usually beats an electric oven when it comes to buying energy. Gas radiators beat electric radiators, although there are some other advantages to having electric radiators like room-controlled heating. If you have solar, electric appliances will always be cheaper as the energy is free. While it may be a big upfront investment, the amount of time it takes for you to make your money back is a fraction compared to other forms of electricity.

A simple thing that applies to gas, wind, or electric is, that no matter what happens, a smaller place is almost always cheaper when it comes to paying your energy bills.

Phone Bill Kill

The phone: a computer in your pocket, messaging system, gaming console, and business tool, and much more.

Unfortunately, it's seen as a status symbol and has become more fashion than function for some people.

If you stand online to upgrade your phone every year for a thousand dollars simply to buy a phone that's almost the same as the phone you have, you're in the fashion category.

Put your brain back on, keep your old phone, go sim free. Only get a new phone when yours is holding you back in some way.

Why upgrade for such tiny innovations? Do you upgrade your television every year? I hope not. Most of the time, these new appliances have bugs that need working out at the launch phase which is another pain.

. . .

If you go sim free and use a company that doesn't take your credit away after a certain period of time, all you really need to pay for is data.

Use a VOIP service or online messenger service for your calls and texts. It's free and it's been free for years and years. The main thing to remember with VOIP is its only free when both you and the other person is online.

Most people's mobiles are always online now, so it shouldn't be an issue for most people. Make sure you have a VOIP provider with emergency calls as an option, even if you only keep it for emergencies.

Popular VOIP providers include Skype, Google Voice, WhatsApp, Vonage, Viber, Facebook messenger and there are lots of other options available. Your home phone line is something else you might want to consider getting rid of. If you have a mobile phone you probably don't really want to pay for a landline as well.

. . .

AT THE MOMENT prices for broadband without the landline are only slightly cheaper and you mind find an alternative company that has phone line and broadband cheaper anyway.

THE OPTION of cutting the phone line will become more attractive in the future, as its likely competition will push broadband prices down and phone line prices will remain the same.

USE a comparison site to find out what works best for you.

SOME PEOPLE MIGHT LIKE to cut the phone line just to stop receiving sales calls and other nuisance calls. Remember that if you work from home, you don't need excessive internet packages on your phone as you have wi-fi.

MONEY – Saving Electronics

YOU DON'T HAVE to cut electronics out of your life to save money. There are many things you can do without changing your lifestyle to save money on your utility bills.

THE FIRST ONE will be to change to all energy-saving light bulbs. There is no reason to have anything else. They are going to be a couple more dollars than others when you go to the store, but they will end up saving you money in the long-term as they last that much longer.

CHOOSE appliances that specifically state that they are energy-saving. This will include dishwashers, fridges, ovens, washers, and dryers. These are incredibly expensive appliances, but you will still need them depending on your situation. When picking them, choose ones that will save energy or at least offer an "energy saving" option to run them. You will be surprised how much the savings add up over time and cover the extra costs from purchasing the higher rated appliance.

FOR YOUR CLOTHES, you should line dry or hang them as often as possible. Still, you won't be able to do this for every load, especially if you have kids who have buckets of laundry on a daily basis. Just make sure to check you're loads in the dryer and open them before completing the cycle. They're likely in there for ten minutes or longer than they need to be, so open up the dryer and check to see throughout to make sure you're not unnecessarily running it.

After this, make sure that you are unplugging things that don't need to be constantly plugged in. Always unplug everything before you go to bed. Does your TV need to be plugged in all night? Not really.

Do you really need to keep your modem on all night? Many appliances won't use electricity if they are turned off, but having others plugged in can still suck up some of your energy and drive up the power bill.

Some people will need to sleep with at least a nightlight on, so anything that you do want to have on as you fall asleep try and use on a timer.

Many people will plug their phone in right before they fall asleep and leave it plugged in all night. Instead of doing this, why not simply try and charge it up before you go to bed? If you are falling asleep with it at 100% then it's not going to die overnight. It's better to unplug the phone over night which helps maintain the longevity of the phones battery so it holds its charge longer.

When using your phone, make sure to keep the brightness as low as you can handle so that it will last longer as well. Turning it down just a few notches might not be noticeable to you, but the duration of your phone's battery life will be. Just because you can charge something up later doesn't mean you shouldn't still try your best to preserve the energy now.

Remember leaving a phone charging after its fully charged can cut the life of your phone's battery considerably. This will increase the amount of money you spend on replacing phones and laptops. Make sure to unplug these types of devices as soon as they are fully charged. You may not notice it right away, but over a lifetime this could save you thousands.

BOSS DOLLARS

The modern businesses office is as cheap as donuts and coffee.

I DON'T KNOW if you have heard, but you don't need an office to get started with your business. If you have a laptop or a phone you're good to go, and if you don't have any of these things, you can get yourself a library card. Borrow the libraries equipment, or borrow a family members or a friend's laptop.

I'M sure you have seen the thousands of people with laptops in every coffee shop and restaurant, well most of them are working. They buy something and set up shop for the day for the price of a drink or their lunch. Some of them work for themselves and some of them work remotely for other companies, it's just the way of the world today.

It can be a good thing to have a real office and a place where people meet face to face, but they are expensive. Remote offices are the cheapest, and every member can work from home which saves them on travel, eating out, and saves thousands of commuting hours for some people.

Some of the biggest companies around today were started at home.

- Jeff Bezos started Amazon out of his garage.
- Microsoft did the same, Bill Gates and Paul Allen started in their parent's garage.
- Roy and Walt Disney started in their uncle's garage working on what ended up being Cinderella.
- Apple was started in a garage by Steve Jobs and Steve Wozniak.
- Harley Davidson was started in a wooden shed, where they were trying to get an engine to power a bicycle, and the rest is history.
- Lotus cars founder Anthony Chapman

started building his first car in a stable next to a hotel.
- Airbnb started when the founders struggling to pay rent decided to rent out 3 air mattresses and throw in the promise of a cooked breakfast.
- LinkedIn started in Reid Hoffman's living room.
- Facebook started in a Dorm room.
- Nike founder Phil Knight started his business out of the trunk of his car.

Here are a few more big companies that all started out of their garage:

- Google
- Hewlett Packard
- Mattel Toy Company
- Dell Computers
- Virgin
- Maglite
- The Yankee Candle Company

As you can see, you don't need to be fancy starting out to make it big in the long run. Save the money and concentrate on the product and service.

. . .

There are usually tax incentives for people who work from home and use a certain portion of their house as a workspace. You can potentially get paid in tax relief by your government to work from home. When you think about applying for this to your whole workforce, the money and time savings can be substantial.

You can employ freelancers before you take on employees, use virtual assistants before you get personal assistants, and work with the self-employed, get part time workers, interns, and hire other companies to offer their services to you. Just build up gradually to full time staff, and lots of them.

If you are looking for remote work, here are some companies that you might like to apply for:

- GitHub – the world's biggest software development platform
- Student loan hero – which helps students work on solving their debt problems
- The United Nation Development Program – helps developing countries around the world
- Study.com – the online free college

- Wikipedia Foundation – non-profit
- content creation platform
- Landi English – E-learning

Remember that remote working allows you to live anywhere with an internet connection. You can choose to live in a cheaper, town, city, country, and get the same pay.

~

THE SOFTWARE NEEDED to run your business used to cost a lot more than it does today, way more.

IT IS NOW possible for most businesses to use completely free software options and take advantage of great cheap high-quality services and platforms. Easy and powerful tools are available to you, it's better than ever for software. Even a few years ago, you could get stuck trying to use difficult software applications.

OKAY, let's look at the office applications first. What you need to know is, they are nearly all free these days.

. . .

You can get the whole google office set up for free. If you don't like some of Google's options you can try using LibreOffice, the free open source suite of office products. Even more amazingly get Microsoft Online Office for free as well.

You can set up your website for free on website.com or use Google's free website for business. Website.com even provides you with a free domain name and hosting it even has a free e-commerce solution. It might be a good idea to use a google website, it's linked with your google my business page and has a search engine on your side. You can use an existing domain name with google but it does not provide one for free.

Saving your data online is the usual way of doing things now, rather than carrying around hard drives all the time. Hard drives and flash drives can still be useful. Passing someone a USB drive is still easier than sending someone masses of data.

Here are some free cloud online data options to use:

- Google Drive 15GB FREE

- BOX 5GB FREE
- OneDrive 5GB FREE (1TB for students)
- iCloud 5GB FREE
- Dropbox 2GB FREE
- Amazon 5GB Free unlimited photos with Prime
- BT Cloud 5-500 GB FREE for BT broadband customers

Every other software you need for business has a free version available if you only take the time to look for it. Email autoresponders such as mail chimp, project management software like Slack, bookkeeping, calendars, to do lists, anti-virus, CRM, screen recording and every other possible thing you need is available somewhere online for free.

WHEN YOU CAN AFFORD something a little better for your e-commerce, I suggest you try Shopify. It has a 1-month free trial and the ease of use is what makes it amazing for e-commerce.

CLICKFUNNELS IS another great option for selling your product and service line up. It makes the selling process into a series of offers so your client gets the most out of your company's promotions at this moment in time.

. . .

I RECOMMEND USING Canva for your simple graphic design platform. It has been great for me as I'm not a professional designer, but Canva makes me look good.

CHEAP AND LEGAL

The legal world is getting cheaper all the time. Mostly due to the online services and excess of qualified legal expertise available.

Getting legally protected with contracts can save you a lot of money in the long run and doing things on a handshake can cost you a fortune.

Having legal documents written up used to cost a lot of money. When you consider most legal documents are the same template printed out for every customer then signed by you.

. . .

Luckily, today, many of the basic legal documents we need are available for free online, so we can print them out ourselves.

Legal document sites to check out:

- Legaltemplates.net
- Lawdepot
- Free-legal-document.com
- Formswift.com
- Uslegalforms.com

If you need a prenuptial agreement you can just use law depot or Rocket lawyer to get their free documents. This saves you money upfront and most of your net worth in the future. If you 100% know your marriage will last until the day you die, you don't need to consider this option.

You can find will's and all sorts of other must have legal documents for free online. You have no excuse not to get your house in order legally. A will can be extremely important for your family if anything happens to you.

. . .

If you care about protecting your family, get a prenup that takes care of everybody and do the same with a will.

If you own property you can find tenancy agreements and all the other necessary documents you need online for free. Property Hawk is a good website for UK property documents.

If you are going through bankruptcy you can use UpSolve to get legal aid, which you will probably need.

If you are looking for Free legal advice just go to RightLegalAdvice.org and they will help you. It's unbelievable that you can get this for free, we are very lucky that these legal services exist.

Seniors advice lines include:

- Legalhotlines.org
- Pension rights center

If you have legal needs that are complex and you

will be needing paid services try using a comparison site.

- Comparelegalcosts.co.uk

I could not find a U.S. legal comparison website at the time of writing this, hopefully there will be one soon.

IF YOU ARE worried about mounting fees you can use a fixed fee service.

- Co-oplegalservices.co.uk

You can use no win no fee lawyers and apply for legal aid in many cases. Use the free online advice services before getting involved with the wrong people.

I HOPE you find the legal world a little bit less intimidating than before and you save yourself some money the next time you have to take care of your legal responsibilities.

RETAIL THERAPY

Anyone who uses retail as a type of therapy could probably use some therapy to stop their retail. A bit harsh but true for some people.

A temporary buzz when buying something you don't need or won't use is a waste of a buzz. If it's something you want then get it if you can afford it. Just don't be buying for the sake of buying. It is a bad habit that destroys a lot of people's finances.

In 1975 pet rock sold 5 million units of the world's dumbest product, and they did it in 6 months. A rock in a package that looked like it was a pet, was sitting in millions of people's houses all across the world, and they are still selling today. That is madness. That is retail therapy at its finest.

LET'S look at some sane ideas for your future purchases.

FIRSTLY, try your best to avoid single-use items, such as paper plates, plastic cutlery, paper towels, plastic straws, etc.

BUY REFILLS RATHER than buying the full product every time. Ink is a great example of this. Air fresheners, coffee, hand wash, salt, and pepper are all cheaper when buying refills.

IT IS USUALLY BETTER to buy hard wearing durable items for the long term. A good pair of shoes last longer than a white pair of trainers. Some cheaply made furniture can be easily broken and is of inferior quality to many second-hand products. You can find second-hand furniture of higher quality made with far superior materials and workmanship if you just take the time to look.

. . .

Swap things with friends and share stuff, it creates bonds and saves a lot of money.

Create a wardrobe of outfits rather than just individual clothes. This is the mix and match method. You can watch tutorials on YouTube, focusing on getting the most outfits possible for the least amount of clothes.

Having lots of outfits from fewer clothes makes your life a lot simpler by shrinking that wardrobe down to something manageable, and again saves you money.

A white shirt goes with almost everything, and some shirts go with almost nothing.

Sometimes buying products from the country they are made in, is way cheaper than buying from countries that just import the products. Sometimes it can be cheaper to buy products from their countries website and pay for the delivery. Clothes from Zara are on average 38% cheaper when purchased in Spain than the U.K.

. . .

TRY generic products rather than big brands at least once to find out what they are like. Occasionally they are even better than the big Brand versions of products. When it comes to generic brand foods, they are often made in the same factory and made by the same company that makes the big brand foods. They are repackaged to increase their revenue.

EVEN AMAZON IS STARTING to make a lot of the sites best-selling products under its own brand name, just like all the supermarkets do, this can save the consumer money on many occasions.

SOME INDUSTRIES PRODUCTS have quicker price drops after release than others, here are some to watch out for.

CARS FAMOUSLY LOSE a lot of value as soon as someone drives them off the lot. Try and find a used car if you can. Computer games drop in value quickly after release and usually are found discounted within 6 months. You can play some 10/10 games that are a little older, if only you have the patience to wait for the inevitable price drop.

. . .

MOST MEDIA LOSES VALUE QUICKLY, DVDs, Cd's, and books are heavily discounted after 12 months and can be found used for low prices.

DON'T FORGET to use the price match option available to you in most large brand stores. They created the price match policy so you could take advantage of the service, so use it when you can.

LOYALTY CARDS and rewards programs are worth signing up to, it's easier than ever to hold all your cards in one place. You can use an app rather than carry around hundreds of plastic cards in a wallet or purse.

WHEN YOU'RE in a store and see a bargain corner always have a look. Many of the items have broken packaging rather than something wrong with the product.

ALSO, look out for ex-display items and offer to buy the display model at a discount if the boxed item has run out.

. . .

SHARE, swap, and up-cycle everything you can. Get things from websites for free and shop around.

MAKE birthday presents if you can't afford to buy anything. Cards, cakes, candles, and you can even use old newspapers as wrapping paper.

IF YOUR FAMILY really needs to make every dollar count, give money as a present. The person who receives the money can decide when to spend the money and not lose any of the value a product might lose.

AT CHRISTMAS, this helps a lot of people because the prices of lots of consumer goods drop straight after Christmas.

MAYBE GIVE a few little presents on Christmas day to make it nice, even though you gave cash as a present.

THE HIGH LIFE

Hotels, Restaurants and Casinos that only leave you half broke.

Double your "living the high life" budget or keep half of what you intended to spend.

The obvious way to get cheaper hotels is book at times of low occupancy. This is different for many places and countries which give you the opportunity to take advantage of this fact.

If you have 2 holidays booked for places in their peak season, you could just swap them around for a lower rate.

. . .

If you do not intend to leave the resort you are staying in, take advantage of their all-inclusive offers.

Longer stays sometimes convert into cheaper holidays. So, it might be better financially to have one long holiday at one resort and take advantage of the long stay discounts available. Multiple holidays are nice but getting a 3-week holiday for the price of 2 separate holidays is nice as well.

Don't be afraid to ask if the hotel has any deals available, they might have a promotion coming up that you can use. Join rewards programs for hotel groups or individual hotels that you go back to frequently.

If you choose to use a credit card, which I don't recommend for most people, you can use a credit card that offers frequent flyer miles and travel rewards to pay for hotels.

. . .

When looking for a holiday, be sure to use the comparison sites such as booking.com and Expedia.

You can price match comparison site prices with most hotels. Look out for hotel coupons on sites like Groupon and take advantage of those great deals.

You can set up price alerts for holidays, flights, and hotels on sites like Kayak.

If you are travelling without a plan or you need a hotel unexpectedly, use one of the cancellation sites to find a good deal. Hotel tonight, Cancelon, Roomer and Priceline express deals are all worth looking at for last minute accommodation.

Restaurants, fine dining and top-quality food can all be cheaper by switching a few things around.

Instead of going out to eat dinner at a fancy restaurant in the evening, go in the morning for breakfast or lunch hours to eat something nice at a cheaper price. Then have cheaper meals later on rather than the other way around.

. . .

It might be a good experience to sign up to be a customer at one of the training restaurants in the universities and colleges. It's something different and you might be eating the food of our future top chef's.

Look out for coupons and special deals by the restaurants of your choice. Keep an eye on sites like Groupon and their competitors.

A rough guide to the world's prices is worth looking into, and we do that by evaluating the food indexes.

The Big Mac Index a list of prices from around the world featuring a product that can be found everywhere and helps us judge food pricing. It's obviously based on fast food but it's still one of the best ways to track average restaurant prices worldwide.

Cheapest Big Mac

- Russia $1.65

- Ukraine $1.94
- Turkey $2.00
- Argentina $2.00
- Malaysia $2.20
- Egypt $2.23
- South Africa $2.24
- Taiwan $2.24
- Romania $2.29

If you look at some of these countries, I'm sure you will find some irony to these findings.

Here are the expensive countries for the Big Mac Index:

- Switzerland $6.62
- Norway $5.86
- Sweden $5.84
- United States $5.58
- Canada $5.08
- Denmark $4.60
- Israel $4.58
- Brazil $4.55
- Australia $4.35

If you're a foodie, I hope the Big Mac Index helps you pick out your next holiday and save you a few bucks.

. . .

LET'S take a look at Casino's the greatest way to go broke and smile at the same time.

MATH AND TIME are against you. The odds are stacked, and you haven't dedicated your life to the game your opponent's play against you.

HOW DO you get to play all day and not lose your hat?

STAY AWAY from games that require no mental effort. You can play these games fast and effortlessly and all you are doing is praying to the luck fairy for a handout.

PLAY games you understand if possible. Imagine playing chess with someone but not knowing how to move the pieces, you're going to lose. Do you want to play this game of chess for money?

IF YOU ARE good at poker then stick to poker, you will lose less money this way. Even video poker is better than the slot machines.

. . .

Craps can last a long time if you're smart. On average, betting $5 a round over a ten-hour period, people only lose only $30.

If you play craps on the slot machine for 10 hours your average loss should be around $630. I would stick to the tables if you want to keep your money.

Stay away from progressive slots, casino games at airports, cruise ships, and resorts. They tend to rig their machines to pay out less as they have no direct competition, unlike Vegas and other gambling destinations. If you are dead set on a gambling vacation, check the local hotels at the casinos. Often times they will offer free hotel stays or upgrades for their gamblers.

Clubs and Bars

Going out to clubs and bars can lead to all sorts of reckless spending, and you have nothing to show for it the next day except a hangover and an empty wallet. Let's look into some decisions we can make before we lose our minds.

. . .

IF YOU HAVE a group of friends that you think will be with you forever through thick and thin, get the first round for everyone and have that delusion ruined by the end of the night.

DON'T BUY rounds unless you're out with the Samaritans at their Christmas party. You very rarely get what you thought you deserved, unless you thought you deserved to be ripped off.

IF YOU DON'T WANT to pay for entry, get there early, or go mid-week when entry will be free or cheap. If you're in a small town this might not be a great idea as there won't be many people out, it's still worth trying once.

DRINK before you go out if you intend to get drunk, and buy the cheaper brands of your favourite drinks.

YOU CAN ALTERNATE DRINKS, one alcoholic drink, one nonalcoholic drink, or just go without to save your money and your liver.

. . .

GETTING home and splitting the fare can be a nightmare. Maybe agree to get an Uber and use their fare split option. If you're alone you might be able to use the Uber pool which picks up people when they already have customers. This saves you money by sharing the fare with a stranger.

LOOK OUT FOR HAPPY HOUR, and coupons and discounts for some clubs and bars.

ALWAYS REMEMBER that if you don't want to go out, don't feel you have to. It can be fun to have one drink and do some dancing, but most of the time, we spend way too much money at the bar when we could be having fun at home.

A CHEAP BEER can be $5 at a bar, when that could be enough to get you an entire six-pack.

NOT GOING out doesn't mean not having fun. Throw parties at your house, have game nights, or watch a movie and play a drinking game with friends. There will always be ways for you to reduce the amount of money you spend and still have some fun.

KEEP WHAT YOU LOVE, SELL WHAT YOU LEAVE

We are going to sell your stuff for life, rather than sell your life, for stuff.

If you have things you love and use, you should keep them, but you should sell the stuff that is unused and unloved. Sell your stuff and get some of those freedom and possibility tokens that we call money in your wallet.

One man's junk is another man's gold, so make sure to check the values of things that have been sitting in drawers for years, you never know how the value of something you purchased years ago may have changed.

. . .

THERE HAVE BEEN tales of people sitting on millions unknowingly. A man living in Toulouse France found a dusty old painting in his attic that turned out to be made by the Renaissance artist Caravaggio. The painting is estimated to be worth between 114 and 417 million dollars. Can you imagine how he felt?

A MAN LIVING in Michigan found out the rock he was using as a doorstop for over 30 years was a meteorite. It weighs 22 pounds and is displayed in the London Natural History Museum and it's valued at approximately $100,000. Not bad for a door stop.

ONE MAN BOUGHT a painting at a flea market for $4 and found something nestled behind a tear in the canvas. It was an original copy of the Declaration of Independence. He went on to sell the document in Sotheby's in Manhattan for 2.42 million dollars. That sounds like the start of a movie, but it happened, wow.

THE CHANCES you have something of extreme value tucked away in a garage is fairly low. It's still worth checking out these things, and have a little bit of fun thinking about it.

. . .

If you do find something that could be valuable, have it checked with professionals rather than just doing a google search.

Let's get back to earth with some everyday products, and where we can sell them.

Collectible items should be sold at auction for the specific type of collector you are targeting.

It is better to sell your old car at a classic car auction if it's a limited edition rather than just a regular auction. This idea applies to all sorts of collectibles.

You can use Craigslist, eBay, Gumtree, and Facebook Marketplace to sell common products such as modern furniture and tech.

Even things like perfume bottles, jam jars, and coffee jars sell on eBay, so it's worth saving a bunch up to sell. Some people use them for crafts and candle making amongst other things.

. . .

Some places have vending machines that pay you to recycle bottles. It's worth checking if there is one in your area, so you can get paid for any recycling efforts you make.

MAKER, PRODUCER VS CONSUMER

Can you make the things you need rather than buy them?

CAN you produce an excess of what you need, that others will pay you for? Perhaps you start to make your own soap instead of buying expensive brands from the store. In the process you might find you're a soap prodigy and everyone wants to get their hands on your product.

CAN you become less of a consumer and become more of a producer? Rather than paying others for their products, find ways to get people to pay you, for yours.

. . .

Food, cosmetics, presents, cakes, candles, furniture, clothes, bedding, garden pots, jam, bread and cleaning products are all things we can make for ourselves. This could be a new hobby and maybe a new business started with your new skill set.

You can use, fix, sell, exchange skills, trade products and use them for gifts. The educational resources to acquire these skills are usually available on YouTube and you will probably be able to find courses in your area at the local college.

Learning new skills can be fun and challenging, it can also give you a sense of achievement and pride in yourself. That could be just as important or more important than any monetary gain.

It's possible to meet new friends at these skill-based courses which are another great reason to go.

You can look for interesting people or businesses that you admire doing the thing you are interested in, see if they have blogs or videos on what they do, and how they make their own products.

. . .

Whether it's a beauty product from a celebrity you love, or your favourite fast food drive thru menu item, if you simply search the title of that, and then "make at home," on Google, you will get a ton of hits. For example, you might search "Starbucks iced coffee at home," and find that there are thousands of tutorials and tips to get your own homemade version.

You will find that these are often better than the product you spend your money on, and you can make your own at a much cheaper price.

Encourage your friends to start on this adventure with you as well. They might be great at making lotion while you are best at creating homemade Snickers bars. Trade these off and save some money! The convenience of store or restaurant-bought things is nice, but the pride you will feel from making them on your own is priceless.

GROOMING AND HYGIENE

Save water, clean quicker, fix your hair, grow a beard and look like captain caveman.

A SIMPLE PLAN for a simple man, soap, clippers, toothpaste, done. As long as your health is taken care of, everything else you might be concerned with is usually vanity.

YOU CAN SHAVE your head fully or give yourself a simple haircut by following instructional videos online. I have to say results may vary but fully shaving your head is almost always a winner.

. . .

SAVE water by using a soapy cloth to wash, then rinse off with another one. If you have long hair use the tap or shower head to rinse off.

THERE ARE lots of cheap toothpaste formulas out there to try, and they are inexpensive and effective. Your grandparents probably used them when they were growing up.

THERE ARE loads of different home-made soaps worth trying to make. It is a simple process and saves you some money.

YOU CAN DO the same with shampoo and conditioner, and you probably already own some of the ingredients to make all these hygiene products.

IF YOU GET good at this and create a nice lineup, maybe you can try to start up a business selling these.

YOU CAN LEARN how to make makeup but some items are more difficult and require experimentation and testing to get the thing right for you. Again, it's still worth a try if you want to make your own.

Apply for free samples of beauty products and get tons of products sent to your home. The emails can get a bit much, but you can always unsubscribe later.

Try generic brands in stores at least once to see if they are worth using.

Keep your razors longer by sharpening them on a pair of jeans, and make sure you brush out all these hairs. Sharpening lessons are on YouTube.

Professional Beauty Care

There is no doubt that hairdressers, nail technicians, and makeup artists have important jobs. They contribute to our economy and provide services to those that want them. However, they can also be rather expensive.

. . .

If you still want to keep your hair dyed, then consider going to a beauty school where it will be cheaper. When it comes to doing your nails, this can all be done from home, it's not something that you need to do weekly or even monthly.

There is a plethora of tutorials on YouTube with people trying to help show others how they can get their hair done. Make friends with hairstylists and see if they will do treatments for you at home. Of course, you will still pay them for their services, but it could be half the price of what might get charged in a salon.

All hairstylists go to the same school as well, so paying way more for treatment in a nicer salon isn't always worth it. The biggest difference will be their amount of experience, but as long as you aren't getting anything too complicated done, then there's no point in having someone who's priced higher do the same job for you.

Next time you do pay to get your hair, makeup, or nails done; pay close attention to the way they do things. How can you take some of their tricks and apply it to your own life?

PET CARE

If you have pets, or you're thinking about getting one, make sure your financial world is in check. Unfortunately, the family pet is usually the first casualty of sudden poverty and given away to the pound or pet charity, and even in some cases just left in the streets to fend for themselves.

I DON'T KNOW how anyone can just let their crying afraid dog loose to roam the streets. It's going to live an awful life, looking for scraps and shelter. Let's try and avoid these things from happening by making it easier to look after your pets in the first place.

. . .

Some of the cheapest pets to own are the goldfish. Unfortunately, that probably won't fulfil any bonding desires you have for your pets. The guinea pig is a nice animal but I'm not sure it's to everyone's taste being part of the rodent family. The leopard gecko is a really easy to look after. It's a small reptile that is cute and can live for around 20 years but remember you have to feed it live animals such as mealworms and crickets. Ant farms are cheap once you have everything set up but they are more of a curiosity to watch rather than a friendly animal to care for. I left some of the most popular cheap pets off the list as they really shouldn't be in a small environment which can shorten their life span from tens of years to just a couple.

The best pet you can have is a dog in my opinion. Man's best friend is a canine, protect and care for each other like family, but even more loyal.

The cheapest dogs to buy and care for listed below takes health care costs and purchase price into account. The prices may vary from country to country and change over time.

- Harrier
- Rat Terrier

- Black and Tan Coon hound
- Platt hound
- Parson Russell Terrier
- American Foxhound
- Miniature Pinscher
- Treeing Walker Coon Hound
- English Setter
- Pug

I would recommend getting your dog from a rescue center, charity, or another type of pet adoption service like adoptapet.com. They help people give their pets a new home for free!

ADOPTING a pet rather than buying stops the encouragement of breeding animals for profit, which leads to unsustainable numbers of pets being born.

GROOM your own animals if you can. Just watch an online tutorial and you are good to go.

CHEAP OR FREE vet care can be found by looking into animal welfare organizations, rescue groups, shelters, and vet schools.

. . .

PET FINDER HAS an animal welfare group search tool worth using.

SOME VET COLLEGES might be able to help you as well. Check the Veterinary Medical Association's list of accredited veterinary colleges where trainee vet's practice, supervised by qualified instructor's and practicing vets.

THERE IS ALSO the Humane Society list of pet financial aid-related organizations. Shop around when using vets and take advantage of payment plans and loyalty cards.

PET INSURANCE IS RECOMMENDED to cover any future problems, if you can afford it. It might save you thousands in the long run. You will find cheap insurance online and cheaper meds online when needed. Sites like Pet Care RX are competitive. You can use a pharmacy checker as well.

ASK about having your dog spayed or neutered to prevent breast cancer, uterine infections, testicular cancer, and perianal tumors.

. . .

MAKE sure to keep up with your annual checks, vaccination schedule, and heartworm prevention. Brush your dog's teeth, exercise daily, and get a healthy dog food to prevent the doctor's bills in the future.

PET PROOF your home from toxic plants, toxic foods, and pest control still lying around, then cross your fingers, you have done all you can. When it comes to dog food, pick the healthiest, and buy in bulk. Buy with friends to get even bigger discounts. Pet food companies make you pay more for buying in small quantities so don't do it.

OTHER WAYS TO Include Animals in Your Life

SINCE PETS ARE EXPENSIVE, not everyone will be able to have one. You can still look for other ways to have an animal in your life! At the end of the day, having a pet is about taking care of an innocent animal. In return, they love you unconditionally and are forever grateful for all that you do!

. . .

You could consider pet sitting if you don't have any pets already. There are plenty of pets out there that need to stay with someone while their owners are at work. They might have anxiety, or they might bark constantly, so their owners want them to be with someone while they're away.

Most of the time, these animals will just sleep during the day, saving their energy for when they're back with their owner. If you work from home and have no pets, this is a great way to make some extra money.

Even if you do have pets, you might still be able to dog-sit depending on which dogs you both have. Simply let the owner know your pet situation and they can decide if it's a good match or not.

Dog walking is a great way to make money without having to do much work. Dog walking is also going to keep you healthy and active, while spending some quality time with the adorable animals.

Pet sitting, and pet walking are all great ways for you to get a sense of what it is like to be a pet owner.

THE WORLD GYM

The title of this chapter refers to the abundance of opportunity for exercise rather than the amount of sport facilities opening all over the globe.

From the park to the beach, from the home gym to the most elite sport centre, there is something for everyone.

When we think of exercise and sport it can be in a very narrow sense. The reality is very broad when it comes to exercise and all movement related practices. There are several motives for taking part in exercise. Some people are exercising for psychological reasons and some are doing it for the physical benefits.

Whether you need to keep exercising to maintain an injury, avoid a health scare, mould your physique into a showstopper, or run a marathon in a certain time for charity, it's possible to do it cheaply, if not for free.

We should all be doing some exercise even if it's just walking. In fact, a long walk is probably one of the most beneficial activities a human can do. Its low stress, very low impact on joints, and works your cardiovascular system to maintain a normal level of fitness that's required for good health. It's not enough for sporting excellence but it's the minimum level of exercise that you do not want to drop below.

Now we have talked about the minimum requirement of exercise to maintain your cardiovascular system, let's explore the myriad of options to step your cardio game up.

If we move logically forward, the next step would be jogging. A pair of running shoes will help protect your joints. There are different theories on what type of shoe people should be wearing. The traditional running shoe saves you impact on your heel, but encourages you to put your heels down. There is a type of shoes without the cushion that encourage you to run on your toes and build up the muscles in your ankles and feet. Either way, you can find a cheap or free way to get out there and start jogging.

ALTERNATIVES TO JOGGING are extensive and appeal to different people in different environments. One of the most beneficial alternatives is swimming as it can work muscle groups not usually activated during cardio. Swimming can be good for people with certain injuries that make it difficult to be on foot for long periods of time. Swimming gives them a chance to be fully active in this alternate environment. Lakes, oceans, and public swimming pools are all around most of us. Just watch out for alligators and get in.

THE BEST WAY TO keep a cardio regimen is to do what is fun for you, and if you can't find anything that you want to be doing again and again, why not rotate through the thousands of options out there. Cycle, row, swim, dance, ski, surf, hike, and play around and experiment, you're sure to find something you like. You will probably end up loving something if you try just the list above.

We still haven't mentioned any team sports or individual sports like football or tennis. We haven't listed the endless fitness regimes, workout programs, exercise classes, cross fit, high intensity interval training, circuit training, cross country, iron man tournaments, martial arts classes, skateboards, roller skates and roller blades, climbing, using trampolines, gymnastics and the list goes on. And it can be split into sub-categories of almost everything we just mentioned.

Exercise is cheap when you consider your options and realize how many hours of enjoyment you get back for your small investment in equipment.

Most exercises have a meditative quality to them, and some sports are so immersive that you cannot be consumed by your everyday thoughts and concerns while playing.

Each person needs something different from their activity, so understand this and don't expect everyone to follow your lead or get the same benefits you experience.

THE EXERCISE REGIME with the most psychological impact for most people is Yoga, not for any reason outside physiology. People associate yoga with spirituality in much the same way people associate meditation with religion and spirituality. Both yoga and meditation can be appreciated by the most pragmatic people only interested in real results with science backing up the anecdotes and individual success stories.

YOGA IS MOSTLY a combination of breathing exercises and positions you must hold for extended periods of time. It is surprisingly difficult and agonizing at times, holding these poses, so you end up only concentrating and feeling rather than thinking. This is a physically demanding workout that has the benefit of slowing your mind down and helping you become less reactive to the stimulus of the world. You become an observer of your own thoughts and the actions of others rather than a reactionary being, not capable of taking everything in and keeping everything in perspective.

. . .

Pilates and Tai Chi have similar aims making you concentrate fully on a movement at all times and not having your mind constantly chatting away. They are all worth a try, but yoga is the most popular with a large amount of people performing the ancient practice every day.

YouTube has lots of free yoga, Pilates, and Tai Chi lessons to go through at your leisure.

Weightlifting and calisthenics on a budget, can it be done? Let's find out. For the sake of raised eyebrows ill start this with a warning to all Mr. Olympia wannabes. There is no cheap way to get that big. The food alone is going to be double a normal person's, and let's all be honest here, hormone replacement is, not cheap.

For the average person looking to get big without injecting hormones and eating for three people, there is some hope of cheap body building.

The first thing I would say is get your nutrition from food rather than supplements. Swap your nutrition deficient diet, for high protein, omega fatty acid rich foods, and get all the colors of the vegetable world into you. Look into bodybuilding food plans and workout with a regimen based on science rather than sales and marketing. If your friends put on extreme amounts of muscle in an unnatural time period while barely training, it's not the latest protein powder making them that way, its steroids.

You can get quite big naturally and buy the equipment for your house, garden, garage, or even leave it down your local park if you fancy risking it getting stolen.

You can get second hand weights for free and cheap, as getting rid of them is a pain, mostly because the weight makes the postage price very expensive and people have to pick them up from your house.

Press ups, sit ups, planches and jumping squats can get you far, while you are waiting for a local bargain.

Look into calisthenics for some great exercises without weights. If you have a pull up bar or there is one at your park or beach, you can do pull ups, chin ups, and other variations that really help improve your physique. Dips are great as well if you have the equipment.

Weights and calisthenic movements are part of bodybuilding and should not be thought of as separate practices, even though many groups act as if they are separate entities.

Some of the best personal trainers and bodybuilders have YouTube channels and websites detailing all their training programs, tips, and tricks.

There are almost no excuses to stay in shape, especially the money excuse.

BABY MONEY

The average cost to raise a child in the U.S. from birth to age 17 is $233,610 which works out to $13,741 a year.

For people earning under $59,200 the average is $174,690 which is $10,275 per year and $856 per month.

The biggest expenses are usually childcare and education. I hope you have good friends and family to help you with babysitting. Maybe someone you know and trust has children and you can take turns to look after each other's children.

. . .

It's not cheap to raise a child no matter what you do, but it can be cheaper if you make some wiser choices.

Always think this thought first, free stuff, hand me downs, presents, borrow, swap, trade. The second thought, used, on sale, in bulk, coupon, done.

Create a gift list for the baby online, and offline for your older family members who can't use the internet yet.

Use this gift list strategically by considering the speed your child will grow, what your priority products are, and how much space you have in your house. Very importantly, helping your friends and family buy the most, with the small amount they can give you. So instead of getting high-end baby stuff from your friends, you get tons of the stuff you actually need.

Your list should only have a certain number of outfits for each age group, this way you have a wardrobe ready to go for years rather than months.

. . .

If you have a basement or attic with lots of space you can ask for lots of bulk nappies and anything else that will be used over a long duration.

Make sure to return the unwanted gifts if you get them within the store return policy window. It can be a pain to go to all these shops, but it's more money towards looking after your child.

Something to keep in mind if you plan on having multiple children is getting a lot of things in unisex so the next child can benefit.

There are some websites helping people share baby clothes amongst other things baby related. So, try and take advantage of this great opportunity that's become available to everyone, sharing is caring.

Always look for convertible gear. Convertible car seats, convertible cribs, and other convertible products that suit your needs.

Convert your dresser into a baby table to save space.

. . .

You can use your sink as a baby tub if it's a decent size and shape to clean your baby.

Keep an emergency bag of baby goods in the car, this way you don't have to drive to the local stores where prices for individual items are much higher.

Reusable diapers can be great for saving money even if you only use them at home.

Remember to always buy your nappies in large quantities. Check who has got a sale on at the time.

Powder formula, versus pre-made, versus mum's natural milk machine. Mum wins for health and price, but it's a personal choice and using formula can make life a little easier. If you can try using powder over pre-made formula all the time, you should save around 50% on the price and it's also easier to carry around.

. . .

DON'T BUY the cute trainers, if you can stop yourself, get them soft booties for a few dollars which should be a small percentage of what you would have paid.

BABIES LEARN to walk barefoot faster than a child who always wears shoes. I'm not sure why that is, but it works.

DON'T FORGET to make sure that you're getting every entitlement and benefit from your employer and the government.

LOOK for support from any local groups. Your library usually has some free classes and information for new parents.

GOOD LUCK with this tough job.

SENIOR PARTY TIME

Stay healthy, and your old age can be full of fun and adventure.

You don't have to slow down just because the other people in your age group are. The inactive retirement is usually a bad idea for your brain and your body, so get out there keep learning and have yourself some fun.

My favorite perk for the elderly has to be all the free travel with public transport. Each country is different but most give people the free public transport option. Just the use of free trains across your country should be enough of an excuse to get out there.

. . .

You can sign up to AARP and Senior discount club to take advantage of all the offers companies use to promote services to senior citizens. If you are not in the U.S. check online for your equivalent service providers.

An organization called NCOS has a tool that helps you find all your entitlements and benefits as a senior citizen.

If you are not signed up to the Affordable Care Act, and still have access to it, do it. It's cheaper healthcare, with the same service. Why wouldn't you sign up for it? It could save your life.

You might be offered tax credits towards solar panels to help you reduce your energy bill. Different schemes exist all over the world, so check your options.

Over 55's housing and loans are offered at substantially lower prices in comparison to normal house prices, and the loans can make your life easier.

. . .

We could not possibly list all the discounts available to seniors across the world but here are some to get started.

- The yellow stone pass for all national parks, including camping $20 a year or $80 forever.
- AARP members save up to $400 on their British Airways flights.
- You can get discounts in lots of restaurants, hotels, cruises, cinemas, theatres, theme parks, even rental cars.

And a lot of the time, all you have to do is say those magic words.

Do you offer a senior discount?

On average your travel is free, your hotel is 20-50% cheaper, and your meals are all 5-10% off.

Have some fun, its cheap.

ALCOHOL, CANNABIS, CIGARETTES, PAIN KILLERS

Why am I helping people get things that might harm their health?

I don't recommend using any unnecessary drug and I wish people could just quit, but it's not that easy and some people don't want to give up. Some drugs have medicinal and anxiety reducing properties that beat the prescription alternatives as well.

Is it a good idea to make addicts even poorer? I don't know, I think it will depend on each individual's unique circumstances and their physical and financial capabilities. If the individual will just spend more on drugs that are killing them, then it's a bad idea. On the other hand, poorer addicts might resort to theft and get into all sorts of problems if their financial situation declines.

I don't feel like there is a right or wrong answer for every person affected so I will continue to present the facts and let you decide the best course of action for your own life.

Beer

I'm using beer as a marker to work out the countries with the cheapest alcohol, some spirits might be cheaper in different countries but the cheapest beer pricing countries can't be a bad rule of thumb.

Did you know the Czech Republic drinks the most beer in the world, out drinking the Australians and Germans?

Here are the cheapest countries to buy beer:

- Ukraine $0.59
- Vietnam $0.59

- Cambodia $0.68
- Saudi Arabia $0.70
- Czech Republic $0.71
- China $0.74
- Panama $0.75
- Macao $0.77
- Serbia $0.77

Maybe not your first pick or the best holiday destinations in the world but it will save you some holiday money if you live near these countries and visit for a vacation.

Cannabis

A controversial plant usually talked about with less nuance than is necessary. It can be both good and bad for people, depending on age, frequency of use, and many other factors.

The medicinal applications for this plant have been proven for some conditions and the ingredients of the plant are used in many prescription drugs.

THE CHEAPEST COUNTRIES TO buy cannabis per gram are listed below:

- Quito, Ecuador $1.34
- Bogota, Colombia $2.20
- Asuncion, Paraguay $2.20
- Jakarta, Indonesia $3.79
- Panama City, Panama $ 3.85
- Johannesburg, South Africa $4
- Montevideo, Uruguay $4.15
- Astana, Kazakhstan $4.32
- Antwerp, Belgium $4.29
- New Delhi $4.38

In Montevideo, Uruguay it is 100% legal, other countries are either partially legal or illegal so look into each country and their laws before going.

CIGARETTES

IF YOU CAN'T GIVE up and you are going broke buying cigarettes, here are the cheapest countries to buy the world's favorite lung cancer makers.

- Kazakhstan $1.05
- Pakistan $1.06

- Vietnam $1.07
- Armenia $1.24
- Ukraine $1.37
- Belarus $1.50
- Colombia $1.53
- Philippines $1.53
- Indonesia $1.75
- Argentina $1.78

When you consider a pack of cigarettes in Australia cost $21 on average and 5 packs cost $105 rather than $5.25 in Kazakhstan you can see a massive difference in the prices worldwide.

PLEASE TRY and give up smoking and add some years to your life, that's the cheapest option.

IF YOU WILL NOT GIVE up try using the filter tips to stop the tar entering your lungs. The tar is what harms your lungs the most, nicotine is the addictive substance. Filters can have a positive effect, even for people that don't give up.

RETAIL MEDICATION

This next section covers all retail medical

spending including painkillers and anxiety related medication. Let's take a look at the top 9 lowest spending countries for medication:

- Sweden $351
- Norway $401
- Netherlands $417
- Australia $427
- United Kingdom $497
- France $553
- Canada $669
- Germany $686
- Switzerland $783

The United States spends around $1011 on retail medication per person. The statistics used for this example did not mention countries in Asia, South America, or Eastern Europe. You might find certain medications cheaper in other countries.

Always use pharmacy checkers and comparison tools online to search out the best deals for all your medical needs.

Whatever you choose to do with the information provided in this chapter, try to take the healthier and safer option for your life if possible.

MEDICAL TOURISM

I wanna live forever I want to learn how to fly, fly!

You should consider flying if your countries health care is not going to cover you in old age. Do they cover your family's hereditary illnesses to the correct levels?

You have got to do what you've got to do. Health should be your number one priority, everyone wants to live a good long life.

Should I stay or should I go now, you have to let me know, should I stay or should I go?

. . .

THAT DECISION IS up to you, luckily Pew research has listed the top countries ranked for best health care services:

- Finland
- Norway
- Sweden
- Switzerland
- Canada
- Denmark
- Germany
- Netherlands
- Australia
- United Kingdom
- United States

As you can see the European countries seem to dominate this list, especially the northern European countries. If you can't stand the cold, Australia comes in at ninth place to save the day, especially if your bones hurt in the cold. Northern Europe would not have been a good option in that case.

ALL THE TOP 10 countries use a single-payer health care system although there are slight differences in each country.

. . .

You might never leave the country your living in now, but you might like to use the cheaper facilities available abroad. You can find cheap dental work, cosmetic surgery, and hair loss treatments in other countries.

You can save tens of thousands on some procedures and get better results in some cases.

If you need cosmetic surgery for any reason, here are the cheapest countries to consider. Of course, always do your research into each hospital before jumping into something as technical as surgery.

- Turkey
- Czech Republic
- Hungary
- Poland
- Lithuania

Turkey is very cheap for many types of cosmetic surgery, putting it clearly at the number 1 spot.

. . .

Dental can be incredibly costly, especially for places like the US, where dental insurance is specialized and rarely included in any type of plan. These are the cheapest places to get your dental work done.

- Costa Rica
- Mexico
- Panama
- Philippines
- Hungary

Dental seems to be cheaper In South America particularly Costa Rica where it is much cheaper. A single implant can cost as little as $800.

When it comes to hair Turkey comes in at number 1 again this time for cheap hair restoration. The best deal available for a FUE transplant for the maximal amount of grafts needed per patient, is priced at only $1574. This might be less than a tenth of the price charged in the world's top cities.

- Turkey
- India
- Ukraine
- Lithuania
- Poland

Do as much research as you can before choosing a hospital and a doctor.

LIFESTYLE CHOICES

Saving money isn't about just putting pennies in a jar. You are going to have to make some serious lifestyle choices if you want to see your cash build up significantly.

Some of us are born into poverty, and others are born into wealth. There are certainly privileges granted to many in terms of finances, but at the end of the day, we all still have to make choices that affect how we will live in the future.

For those not born into wealth, it's going to be a lot harder. It's not fair, but it's going to be a struggle compared to those that were born into riches and financial education.

. . .

Don't worry about your starting point, we all face tough challenges in life whether born into riches or not, the financial struggle can be the push you need to gain self-discipline and make a success of all parts of your life.

Look back on your life and reflect on your experiences to see what might have led you to have the spending habits you have now.

When you see the reality of how your money habits were created, it's easier to tackle the issues that face you in your future.

Our spending habits are usually copied from parents and siblings, we unconsciously adopt their strategies for using money even if their situation was different.

We need to adapt, rather than adopt strategies that do not make sense for ourselves and our own unique situations.

. . .

Each generation has its own opportunities and drawbacks so you can't expect to copy the previous generation and get the same results.

Minimalism

Minimalism is a lifestyle in which one chooses to not live beyond their basic needs.

You might consider studying other forms of philosophy, such as stoicism, that fall in line with these kinds of lifestyles.

You might have heard of minimalism as a trend, or maybe you know it from the art world.

Minimalism became popular in the early 60s. Art at the time was very academic and filled with its own hierarchies. Basically, if you weren't a certain kind of skilled artist, with the right education, you weren't considered as artistic.

. . .

IN RESPONSE TO THIS, many artists started creating more abstract pieces. This is where minimalism was born.

NOW DAYS it's known more for being a lifestyle where living with few things and fewer needs is the goal.

MANY PEOPLE THINK that you will have to throw your things away and leave nothing but a few outfits and a mattress on the floor but that is not the truth. If that's what you want though, go for it!

IN REALITY, it only involves getting rid of everything that doesn't make you happy. We keep so many things around that have very little value to us.

HAVING to maintain and clean the things we have take's time energy and money, just dusting around lots of things piled up around the house is hours of labor that could serve you, or pay you somewhere else.

. . .

How many items do you have boxed up in your home or sitting in storage? Aside from Christmas and Halloween decorations, nothing should just be sitting in your garage all year untouched.

It's important to have memories like family photos, or even old invitations or concert tickets. These should be minimal, however. You can store all your photo albums digitally rather than taking up lots of space. All those albums, saved in the cloud, you don't even need a memory stick.

Minimalism isn't about having no stuff at all. Just get rid of what doesn't make you happy. If you love movies, books, and records, keep your discs around.

Go through things and get rid of anything that's an obligation. You might have old gifts around that you hate from distant relatives just because you feel too guilty to give them away. Give them to someone who actually wants them and make someone happy.

Perhaps you have half-finished projects lying around that you haven't been able to get finished, it's ok to give these away, throw them out, or sell them.

. . .

Once you start to getting rid of some of the stuff you don't need, it becomes easier to do this in the future, and you will become less of a hoarder, which is a good thing.

Minimalism can save you money, time and reduce the stress of having an overcrowded overstimulating space.

Quality Over Quantity

It can be helpful to consider the quality of a product over the quantity or price of some products.

You might want to choose quality over low price in situations where the product declines with time, and the quality item remains in good condition for longer and ends up saving you money in the long run.

. . .

This is something that you will want to consider with all types of purchases, the long term effects of buying inferior products can be more trouble and expense than they are worth. Sometimes research and a judgment call is the only defence you have against a bad customer experience.

When it comes to your health, home and finances. Try to choose quality over low price as often as you possibly can.

Skip the Lottery

There's nothing that someone who's lived in poverty for a while might be more hopeful than a big lottery win.

The lottery is a fantasy that keeps the middle and lower-classes focused on spending their money on a chance, rather than getting a financial education and working for a more realistic and substantial future.

. . .

BILLIONS ARE SPENT every single year on the lottery, but how much have you ever actually won? When it comes to scratch-off tickets, there's a good chance you've one a dollar or two in the past. Lottery companies know that small wins are important to keep the customer happy so they keep coming back.

IT WORKS in a similar way to slot machines.

GUESS WHO'S BUYING the most lottery tickets? Those who are living in poverty. We can't let this happen anymore.

SOME LOTTERIES PROCEEDS go to charity, that's great but the majority of people buying the tickets are living from pay cheque to pay cheque. Is it better to stop gamblers being seduced into super low odds games just to make one individual a millionaire, and build a local park?

A LOT of the lottery tickets are paid for out of social security cheques then redistributed to the lottery which gives money to charity and makes a random person a millionaire. Is this a good thing? I don't know.

. . .

You can still participate every once in a while, if you want. It can be fun to enter raffles at bars or to play games in Vegas. However, it's important that you keep up the right mentality and stay focused on saving your money, not spending it all on a small chance.

The future of your finances should never be based on terrible odds.

TIME IS MONEY

The Time Cost of Money

We have all heard of the phrase "Time is Money" but what does that really mean to you specifically. Most people will think of it as their hourly rate or wage but some will think beyond this.

What is the cost of you not working that extra hour over a year?

What is the cost of not investing in new skills and knowledge?

. . .

WHAT IS the time cost of not investing your savings?

ONE OF THE most common mistakes when it comes to time and money is working on things at home that can be paid for such as gardening, when you can earn more per hour while a gardener works on your garden.

EXAMPLE: You are a painter working for $30 an hour, you need to clean your house for an hour or pay someone $10 to clean for you. It would make logical sense to work the extra hour painting for $30 and have someone clean your house for $10, this way you keep $20 more for the same amount of time working.

IF YOU CAN MAKE money at a higher rate than all home related tasks you should hire someone to do them for you, keep working on what you do best, and get well paid for doing it.

MONEY GROWS ON WHAT?

Let's have a look at some of the common negative beliefs around money. Maybe you have some of these. If our ideas about money are wrong, we will keep going backwards into negative patterns of spending and waste. You can change these ideas to something more realistic and helpful for your future.

The meek shall inherit the earth.

You don't inherit the earth; you live in it.

The rich man has as much chance of going to heaven as a camel trying to go through the eye of a needle.

That seems harsh, as money is made by giving

services and products in exchange for money, and requires the rich to dedicate their lives to giving.

The rich made their money at the expense of the poor, they are all criminals.

Some rich people are criminals, some poor people are criminals, which demographic has the most crime, the poor. Criminal activity is actually very low amongst the rich, and business is overseen by laws that punish these types of business people.

Money is the root of all evil.

Neither excess or lack of money actually point toward higher levels of criminality and aggression in populations.

The Gini index tracks inequality data, and has found that inequality increases violence as young males fight for status. Apparently, the root of all evil is an uneven playing field, and the dis-advantaged players are willing to commit violence to ascend to a higher level.

The rich get richer, the poor get poorer.

There is an element of truth to this, but the devil

is in the details. The reality is, the financially educated get rich and the financially illiterate get poorer. Have you seen these lottery winners and sports stars lose millions in a few years? They were rich and they certainly didn't get richer, and the opposite is also true. Roughly 80% of millionaires are 1st generation self-made millionaires and that number is increasing every year.

It's selfish to want a lot of money.

It's more selfish to be poor, than want a lot of money. Who can you help with no money? What great cause can you fund? You should be trying to get money to help everyone around you.

Mo Money, Mo Problems.

You will have problems either way, rich or poor, but you can get the best medical care, take time off, and have choices when you are rich.

Money can't buy me happiness.

Maybe, that's true but poverty is definitely not buying happiness either. It's not buying anything.

. . .

If you feel guilt, shame, embarrassment or any other negative emotion about having money, it's because it's linked to a negative belief.

Try your best to search your feelings and find these false ideas you have about money. The ideas probably come from your parents, and they probably learned the same ideas from your grandparents.

If you can free your mind from these negative beliefs, you can follow proven processes to a better life.

It still won't be perfect, but it will be easier.

SAVE THE WORLD A TRILLION DOLLARS

Saving money is not just for yourself. It's for your family, your community, your country, the human race. They all need YOU!

THE BUTTERFLY EFFECT of all our actions creates unseen consequences across the world.

THE CONSUMER DEBT of a nation solely relies on the personal responsibility of individuals to take actions that benefit themselves and the wider community.

WE DON'T NEED another recession like in 2008 or depression as we had in the 1930s, and if we don't want to see these types of events happen, we have to change.

We can't take out loans we don't understand just because someone says we can have the loan. We have to be educated enough to make decisions based on some fundamental understanding of the things we sign up for, and the personal risk involved.

Don't just get out of debt to live month to month, or save money just for the sake of saving. Become intentional with your resources as if each dollar you received were a token towards freedom, and choices, and wider contribution.

Each positive individual action echoes through humanity by commerce, supporting the family and paying taxes, to provide for the poor, protect civilization, and fund a better future for all the citizens.

Some would like to argue this point, but I would refer you to the history section of the library. Your life expectancy should be enough to be thankful for, every day.

. . .

If you have the will to take it upon your shoulders and commit to an optimal way of living, and the masses follow your lead, we can avoid conflicts, spend more on the world's problems, and solve them before they lead to unnecessary tragedy.

The world will never be perfect, but each step towards a positive goal sets us up for a better future.

And for each and every person, it starts with putting your own house in order.

IDEALLY

Ideal Scenarios

WHAT IS the ideal scenario for your life? I don't know, only you can know what that is.

THE IDEAL SCENARIO for your expenses should be fairly similar for all of us. We all want to spend nothing for our recurring expenses, and even get paid from the things that used to cost us money.

I IMAGINE this scenario would appeal to 99% of the readers.

. . .

YOUR RENT IS PAID for by letting out a room that has a separate entrance, and you even make a profit each month.

YOUR UTILITIES ARE PAID by the solar and wind power you had installed by a government scheme, or you paid for them to be installed. And sometimes you even get paid by the grid for sending electricity.

MOST OF YOUR food is grown in your garden and the rest of the food you buy is cheap and tastes great. You even make some money from the excess food you grow.

YOUR HEALTHCARE IS FREE.

YOUR COLLEGE or university is free.

YOUR CAR PAYMENTS are a thing of the past, you are living close to everything you need, or you work from home.

ENTERTAINMENT IS FREE, if you want it to be.

. . .

Travel is free if you want it to be, you just have to pack your food. You are getting paid by renting your whole home while you are gone, and making money while traveling.

Your water bill is cut down to a tenth of what it was, which should be very cheap.

You have way less stress, so much more free time, and a large amount of savings in the bank. Life is good.

HERE'S BIG SPENDER

The Difference Between Being a Thoughtless Spender or an Optimal Spender

YOUR LIFE WILL BE the result of your decisions, so your decision-making skills, and your level of awareness can change everything.

YOUR FINANCIAL DECISION-MAKING skills are a big part of your life whether you focus on it or not, even if you care or don't care about it. You still get to live with the consequences.

THE DEPLOYMENT of capital is a skill you hear used by people like Warren Buffet when talking about buying companies and shares. It is the most fundamental skill of investing your money for greater return.

It might seem like you don't need to be an expert at deploying capital but that is not true. The less money you have, the more skill is needed when using up each dollar.

Each dollar can acquire a certain amount of resources.

There is a maximum amount of resources gained per dollar spent and a least amount of resources gained per dollar.

Imagine the amount of gold you would gain with a dollar versus the amount of water a dollar can buy you. A speck of gold dust or the thing that keeps us alive. $1 of tap water equates to 35,853oz. We only need so much water to survive, but 64 ounces a day is recommended for good health.

. . .

YOUR JOB IS to acquire quality resources with the limited money you have available to you, and try not to waste the power of your dollar.

THE ACCUMULATED effect of stretching your dollar to its greatest potential is the money saving and wealth building strategy that sets you free and hopefully brings you wealth in your future.

IF YOU MAKE the most of your dollars one month and save a thousand dollars that's great. If you do that for 5 years, that's $60,000 saved just from saving a thousand a month.

OPTIMIZE YOUR SPENDING, because each dollar lost is a freedom token lost. Increase your decision-making skills and your optimal spending skills increase helping you keep your money.

Assets Versus Liabilities, Investments Versus Sinking Ships

WHAT IS AN ASSET: An asset is a resource with economic value that will provide a future benefit.

. . .

What is a Liability: Liabilities are legally binding obligations that are payable to another person or entity.

The rich mostly buy assets, things that increase in value and pay them from the profits created.

Businesses, investment property, collectables, machinery and other income generating assets.

The middle class usually buy things that hold or increase in value slowly over time.

Buying your own home, luxury cars and boats can be a gift or a curse to your pockets, this really depends on your eye for a good deal. Generally these things lose or increase value at a fairly slow pace.

The poorest members of our society have little choice but to buy liabilities, which will lose value and cost more to purchase or rent over extended periods.

. . .

Buying anything with a credit card that charges high fees can be classified as a liability.

When it comes to the things that people purchase, the differences seem minimal but the long-term outcome of those seemingly small differences can change everything.

Try to buy income generating assets and try not to buy liabilities that lose you money.

If you do this for an extended period of time you should reap some financial rewards.

THE NEXT LEVEL, BEYOND SAVINGS

Any increase in your income creates less need for savings, as long as your expenses don't increase at the same level.

WHEN YOU HAVE SAVED some money, the opportunity to make more becomes available. It is a positive loop that helps you create wealth over time.

EVEN IF YOU have a full-time job, your money can be out there working for you in a thousand different ways. This is called investing.

THE FIRST RULE of investing is, never lose money. So, find something you understand to invest in. The financial side of what you try must be understood completely. Try to get as educated as you can in all aspects of investing and deploying capital.

Sometimes your returns will be better if you can control the investment and improve it yourself, rather than putting your money into other people's businesses, where you have no control and can't take advantage of opportunities.

A good example of this would be purchasing a house and renovating it. I'm not suggesting you do that, but you can consider this option. Research and educate yourself in whatever you do, to be safe.

You are your greatest asset and increasing your awareness, knowledge, and skills can be the ultimate investment, even if it does not pay off financially.

I know this is a book on saving, and I know some will think it's not relevant, but I feel it would be foolish to not reveal the next step in your journey to financial success. You can have a good life from just saving, but most of us can't get filthy rich just by saving.

. . .

You have to do something with the money, if you want to know how the other half, or the 0.1% live. Start businesses, learn high-income skills, buy businesses and other income producing assets, and live the dream.

No one can take your skills and knowledge from you so invest in yourself, expand your world of possibilities, and take some action.

Virtue by Frugality

A wise man does not judge a man by his words but by his actions. Will your actions change you as a person?

The gift of intentional living and having a life you are creating rather than participating in, will be more fulfilling and can change many aspects of your life.

Thomas T Munger said, "The habit of saving itself, is an education, it fosters every virtue, teaches self-denial, cultivates the sense of order, trains to forethought, and so broadens the mind."

We might be able to have more money in the bank by saving, but more importantly, we will have more inner strength for whatever challenge comes next. If self-discipline can be trained using the practices of frugality, the mindset of self-control and planning for a better outcome in all aspects of life is possible.

Your health, wealth, relationships, and happiness have a much higher chance of success because you are trying to steer the boat that is your life, rather than being swept along by life waves.

Simple habits, better choices, positive sacrifice, all trained into your mind by practicing how you use your resources for a greater result.

Elon Musk

Elon Musk decided to see if a $30 food budget could get him through a month.

He bought mostly hot dogs and oranges in bulk and would occasionally switch it up with some pasta and jarred tomato sauce. He pulled it off.

This helped give him the confidence to believe he could be an entrepreneur and afford to live in the U.S. no matter what happened. He said, "it's pretty easy to make $30 a month so I'll probably be ok."

. . .

THIS EXPERIMENT HELPED RELIEVE the pressure from a young Elon and helped him focus on his loftier goals like, starting an electric car company and sending people to Mars. Elon Musk is one of the greatest entrepreneurs on the planet and might not have got to this position so quickly if he had not decided to make a saving experiment.

BRANDON

A 23-YEAR-OLD GOOGLE employee named Brandon saves money by living in the back of his 16-foot 2006 Ford truck. He parks in the Google parking lot and uses Google's facilities for all his basic needs. His only expenses are his $121 a month insurance.

LIVING in the truck saves Brandon at least $2000 a month and saves him commuting to work while paying off his student debt.

BRANDON IS SAVING 90% of his income at 23 years old. I think he is going to be ok.

. . .

Sarah Carter

If you live in San Francisco this story might interest you.

23-year-old Sarah Carter decided to buy a boat for $9,600 to live on. This helped her to save money on rent, which is around $3,500 a month in San Francisco for just a 1-bed apartment. Her total housing cost for the month living on the boat comes to $350, a ten-fold saving. She will sell the boat for the same price if she decides to move elsewhere.

San Francisco is one of the most expensive places to live, and this is a great way to drive down rental payments.

Benjamin Franklin

Benjamin Franklin the great founding father is known in America as the father of frugality. He even coined the phrase, "a penny saved is a penny earned." Franklin stayed away from the lavish lifestyle and dressed plainly and ate simply.

. . .

He surrounded himself with like-minded people who lived below there means. Franklin became a self-made millionaire by the time he was 42.

Hetty Green

Hetty Green, a bad example of frugality. The Guinness book of records gave her the title of the world's greatest miser. She was born into a wealthy family but came from frugal family culture and religion.

Hetty chose to never wash in heated water and never even had a heating system in her home. It must have been cold in there, especially every winter in New York.

She had only one plain black dress that she wore every-day and only cleaned specific areas of the dress, to save on soap.

Hetty's son broke his leg, she took him to the free clinic reserved for the poor, to avoid the doctor's fees. This mistake led to poor Ned eventually having his leg amputated. Hetty even refused treatment for herself, just before she died to avoid the $150 price tag.

THIS IS A CAUTIONARY STORY, Hetty is the proof you can go too far with saving, and you need to know what's important. I would say life and the health of your child is an obvious starting point.

RONALD READ

ANOTHER HERO of saving is a local legend from Brattleboro, Vermont called Ronald Read. He used the classic saving tricks, like driving a second-hand car, and gathering his firewood, but he took it to extremes as well. He used safety pins on his shirts when the buttons fell off.

HE WOULD EVEN WALK a mile to save on the parking meter.

HE WAS A GAS STATION ATTENDANT, and a janitor after that until he retired at 75.

. . .

When he passed away at 92 it was revealed that he was, in fact, a millionaire and had accumulated over £8,000,000 by investing wisely in the stock market.

His family did not have any idea about his vast riches and the only thing that could have given them a clue about his financial savvy was his reading of the financial times.

His simple spending habits and financial knowledge paid off, and upon passing he left $6,000,000 to the hospital and library.

A wise man does not judge a man by his words but by his actions. Will your actions change you as a person?

THE GIFT of intentional living and having a life you are creating rather than participating in, will be more fulfilling and can change many aspects of your life.

THOMAS T MUNGER SAID, "The habit of saving itself, is an education, it fosters every virtue, teaches self-denial, cultivates the sense of order, trains to fore-thought, and so broadens the mind."

. . .

We might be able to have more money in the bank by saving, but more importantly, we will have more inner strength for whatever challenge comes next. If self-discipline can be trained using the practices of frugality, the mindset of self-control and planning for a better outcome in all aspects of life is possible.

Your health, wealth, relationships, and happiness have a much higher chance of success because you are trying to steer the boat that is your life, rather than being swept along by life waves.

Simple habits, better choices, positive sacrifice, all trained into your mind by practicing how you use your resources for a greater result.

REVIEW

☆☆☆☆☆

To Leave an honest review please use the link below.

HTTP://WWW.AMAZON.COM/REVIEW/CREATE-REVIEW?&ASIN=B08N2R4SYG

I CAN'T EXPRESS how much we appreciate getting feedback and reviews. They really help to keep the book alive. Thank You so much for reading.

- Scott McDowell

AFTERWORD

If I Could Only Give You One Thing

I would free your mind, take away your false fears, and make you believe in yourself.

A terrible thing to find out in life is that people dumber, less talented and lazier are living the life of your dreams, just because they believed in themselves and didn't give up.

You are enough!

This life of freedom and peace of mind isn't just reserved for other people. It's available to anyone willing to keep fighting for what they want.

You can have savings, businesses, cars, houses, holidays and an amazing life.

As Jim Rohn said, "If you will change, everything will change for you".

You can't be limited by the world you see around you, the people you know, or the media you consume.

This is a world full of unbelievable opportunities and it needs you to stand up for what you want out of life.

What is the point of quietly tip toeing to your grave?

This life is for living and trying out all the great things it has to offer.

Write down what you want from your life and make a plan for it.

If it takes ten years to do it, let it take ten years, it's better to have ten years running towards your dream than 10 years just getting by.

Unless you're reading this from in prison, you're not inside a cage. You can walk your way into another situation, another job, another life.

The chains holding you back from moving towards a better future are in your mind. Are you waiting for the right moment? There won't be a perfect moment. Are you hoping someone will put their life on hold and help you? You're going to be waiting for a long time.

Do what you can, with what you have, even if you don't have a lot.

Everyone has to start somewhere, so start where you are and become resourceful.

If we become resourceful, we can find all the things we need to get started.

The best resource in the world is resourcefulness.

No money? Save it, earn it, raise it, partner with someone who has it, loan it, trade for it, find a way.

No skills, learn, train, apprentice, volunteer, find a job, a coach, find a way.

You see it all just takes one step at a time towards your goal.

How do you eat an elephant? One bite at a time.

I hope you realize that your life is in your own hands and you can change something, at any time.

Get busy living.

Thanks for reading.

www.ingramcontent.com/pod-product-compliance
Lightning Source LLC
La Vergne TN
LVHW010319220926
848484LV00004BB/794